Contents

IT Infrastructure Library

IT Service Management Case Studies

HMSO: LONDON

Acknowledgements   The assistance of authors from various consultancies
who provided these case studies for CCTA, is
acknowledged. Annex A gives a profile of each of the
consultancies involved.

PRINCE® is a registered trademark of CCTA, the Government Centre for
Information Systems

© Crown Copyright 1996.   Published by permission of Stichting EXIN under licence
from the Controller of HMSO.
Applications for reproduction should be made to
HMSO's Copyright Unit.

ISBN: 0 11 330676 8

For further information regarding CCTA products and services please contact:

CCTA Library
Rosebery Court
St Andrews Business Park
Norwich
NR7 0HS
01603 704704

1 Introduction

1.1 Purpose

The main aim of the IT Infrastructure Library (ITIL) has been well documented. It is to facilitate improvements in efficiency and effectiveness in the provision of quality IT services and the management of the IT infrastructure within any organisation. Each ITIL book provides best practice guidance on how to plan, implement and review a certain element of IT service management. But people like to read about the problems other people encounter when using the guidance in real life situations and how they overcame those problems.

This book contains ten case studies, provided by companies that use ITIL as a basis for their IT service management consultancy and software tools. The studies are based on their experiences either when working on individual projects or, in one case, of experience accumulated over a large number of projects. Organisations at all stages of implementing IT service management, from planning to review, or organisations having already done so, will find the case studies useful when formulating their approach, or when looking to improve the quality of their existing systems.

1.2 Audience

The obvious, and probably the main, audience for these case studies is IT Service Managers and managers with responsibility for delivery and support of essential elements of IT service management. They should also prove of interest and relevance to those with responsibilities for outsourced IT service provision; to Quality Managers; to applications developers; and to IT systems auditors. As well as those involved in the provision of IT service, those on the receiving end, ie business managers, may find it useful to read about the problems experienced and the benefits achieved by other organisations in the delivery and receipt of IT service management.

The studies demonstrate the range of different environments within which ITIL has proved its value and relevance in private sector organisations, local and central government and utilities. Geographically, the ten studies are split equally between the UK and the Netherlands, those countries currently making most use of ITIL guidance, although this situation is changing

7

rapidly as ITIL is taken up in countries around the world.

1.3 Structure of this volume

Chapter 2 describes how the case studies have been assembled.

Chapters 3 to 12 contain the ten case studies.

Annex A gives a short profile of the consultancies that provided the case studies. These and other companies can provide services and products in support of IT service management. Annex A does not constitute an 'approved' list of ITIL service providers.

A chapter outlining other related guidance and useful information and a Glossary of terms used in this volume are also provided.

2   Overview

This book provides a set of ten case studies that will be of interest and use to organisations involved with or contemplating an approach to IT service management as contained in the IT Infrastructure Library (ITIL).

The case studies have been selected to show how the contributors set about tackling problems they met when implementing certain elements of IT service management in a live situation. They are intended to present a complementary picture to the more theoretical approach contained within the mainstream ITIL books. As such they represent a more pragmatic view, concentrating on problems encountered and overcome and with the compromises needed to achieve a broadly ITIL conformant application within a real organisation.

The case studies clearly reflect the different organisations who have prepared them and the wide variety of organisations on whose experience their work is based. Only the very minimum of editorial change has been made to the case studies submitted for this book. This minimalist approach has been a deliberate act to preserve as far as possible the directness of the experience recounted.

Some of the case studies have been written so as to keep the source organisation anonymous. Others name those concerned – both organisations and individuals. We have been pleased to see this; it allows positive identification of two elements of implementing IT Service Management (ITSM) that cannot be put across convincingly in the mainstream ITIL work:

- service management is not only about IT equipment and organisational procedures – it is more about people, ITSM people providing a service to their users and customers

- the success (or failure) of an ITSM initiative often (arguably always) depends on the enthusiasm and drive of a single manager to make it happen. Without a 'champion' willing to put their reputation, and perhaps their job, on the line to support and drive the project, then it is less likely to happen.

Reinforcement of this is evident from the frequency with which the case studies are written in the first person. When a case study starts out with 'What we wanted to do,' then the reader is already confident of a happy ending.

2.1 **Fit with CCTA guidance**

The approach to implementing IT service management, contained in ITIL, is based on perceived contemporary best practice. However, best practice is evolutionary, especially in an area such as ITIL which combines IT and management. These case studies document some situations where it was necessary to adapt the ITIL guidance to fit with the particular organisation and its circumstances. This can be taken as an indication of ITIL's adaptability: it does not rely on a dogmatic 'all or nothing' approach. It is, and indeed always has been, a tool for managers – documenting best practice, offering a structure for organisations, but allowing IT service management professionals to function and bring their skills to the particular circumstances they find.

2.2 **Synopses**

ITIL as an agent for change – 1
(Chapter 3)

ITIL was introduced into an IS organisation threatened by competition in supplier choice for its services to the client business. Quality improvements to its processes and customer focus were necessary for its survival. The keys to success shown in this study were implementation of ITIL (but avoiding a bureaucratic approach), responsibility upon all staff to improve processes and good communications throughout the quality improvement programme. Most importantly, success came by taking as a starting point the gap between the customers' needs and the capabilities in the organisation. Having survived, the organisation intends to *further improve* its service delivery and customer responsiveness.

ITIL as an agent for change – 2
(Chapter 4)

An electricity supplier's central IT department was faced with the threat of outsourcing. A review by ITIL experts showed that the department was not satisfying end-users' requirements and had poor contact with its customers. Internal management had not tackled control and reporting issues.

A quality improvement programme was set in train to improve service management. The department was re-organised, work group specific procedures set up and training given.

Some improvement has enabled the department to survive, but the customers' expectations have been raised and must now be met! Help Desk and problem management procedures are working well, but implementation of other ITIL service management processes needs to be completed and service level agreements with the customers formalised.

Implementing a systems managed environment (Chapter 5)

Following the acquisition of this medium-sized company in the financial and pensions sector, strong pressure was placed on its IT department by the larger company to implement ITIL best practice. The mission was to implement a systems management environment for the provision of computer facilities to the company to measured levels of service – in three months.

The effort and resource to do this was underestimated and things did not progress quickly enough until a Service Manager was appointed to see through the implementation.

Delivering an application support and maintenance service (Chapter 6)

The provider of third party application support and maintenance services has incorporated the ITIL approach to provide a means of continually improving its effectiveness and efficiency, and to follow recognised standards.

The company aims to install an application support service tailored to match each customer's environment. This case study highlights issues in implementing each ITIL element.

Technological change, market testing and agency status (Chapter 7)

This is a case study about a government department's IT directorate, and the way in which it responded, in service management terms, to three changes drivers: technological advance, market testing and executive agency status. Initially, only one division of the directorate was targeted for implementing service management, but the interdependencies with other divisions and the need to create a new relationship with the directorate's customers suggested the need to implement each ITIL function in turn across the whole organisation.

Service management implementation (Chapter 8)

A service culture has been created within this local authority's IT department. User dissatisfaction with computer response times and a haphazard approach to change requests had resulted in 'total disillusionment with IT'. The new manager of the department started to introduce a service management culture, and then discovered ITIL, which became the guiding light for achieving this aim. The organisation responded to the threat of compulsory competitive tendering by ordering an external review of the health of its service management. This showed up weaknesses which were addressed, through the further implementation of ITIL functions and training.

Disaster recovery planning (Chapter 9)

This case study starts with the contingency planning for the local authority's financial services computer systems. The priority was to have disaster recovery in place for mainframe systems, then a more complete business continuity plan was developed, with external advice.

The IT department is now developing its *intelligent customer* role as a facilitator and enabler of IS/IT. The focus has moved out beyond mainframe contingency planning into the office systems generally and the intention, over time, is to implement business continuity planning for all of the authority's IS.

ITIL support for IT service quality improvement (Chapter 10)

There was pressure on the IT department of a major telecommunications company to do more with less – to an improved level of quality! A search for methods for improving the entire service lifecycle ended with ITIL. But ITIL would only be taken on if it proved flexible and adaptable to the organisational structure of the IT department, and provided the means to build in quality without incurring more staff overheads.

The department focused first on processes in order to bring about overall service quality improvements. A model (*Implementation of Process-oriented Workflow*™) was defined to place ITIL functions within the circle of quality improvement. When the processes, process boundaries, roles and responsibilities were clear, it became easy to build procedures and work instructions, drawing on the guidance contained in ITIL modules. An external audit recorded a high level of ISO9002 compliance. The challenge was then to extend implementation of the model into the End User Service Department …

Justifying and implementing support tools for ITIL (Chapter 11)

ITIL enables IT specialists to adapt to technological, political and market developments. The IT department of an industrial insurance board faced competition as a supplier of IT services to an organisation whose own customers are now free to choose where to obtain insurance services. The IT department started by seeking configuration management and Help Desk tools and found it was on the trail of ITIL.

Measuring advantages gained from using ITIL (Chapter 12)

The final case study describes the benefits of successful implementation of ITIL in the computing centre and infrastructure department of a large organisation implementing social legislation. There have been frustrations along the way, but the ITIL approach has come to be of vital importance to the department, focusing as it does now not just on software, hardware and networks, but on providing services to customers that meet their specific requirements and anticipating the impact of new developments on future requirements.

IPW is a trademark of the Quint Wellington Redwood Group and PTT Telecom Automation

ITIL as an agent for change - study 1

3   ITIL as an agent for change – study 1

*This case study was provided by
The Pink Elephant Group*

3 ITIL as an agent for change – study 1

3.1 Where we started from and what triggered the change

How do you get twenty individual groups of IS staff to share one vision?

No, it isn't a children's playground joke, but a problem which was costing us lots of money and threatening us with the loss of our customer base.

Let me set the scene. We work in the IS division of a multi-national chemical company. The company employs twenty thousand people in twenty international locations and is rapidly expanding through acquisition of smaller chemical concerns.

We had been through a consolidation exercise in which the IS units, which were fragmented throughout the organisation, were brought together under the control of one umbrella IS division. This division alone consisted of six hundred staff. The intention was to give IS a standard vision and direction.

However, despite this central control, each IS unit interpreted the IS policy differently, with the result that there was no uniformity in direction for IS.

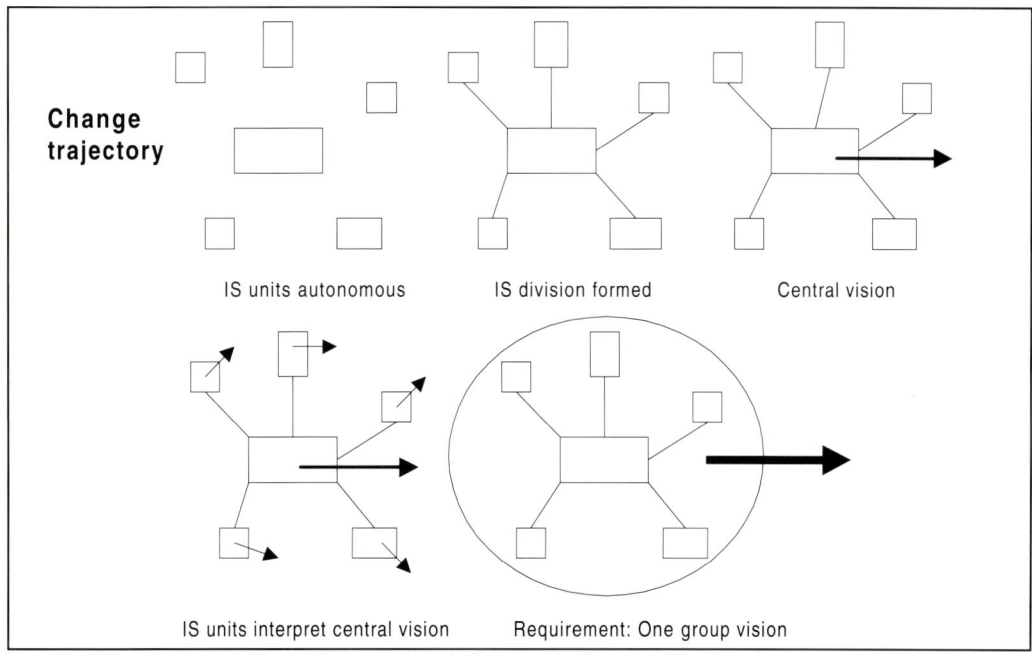

Figure 3.1: Direction and vision of IS

We also had a major shift in company policy to contend with; it had been decided to concentrate on 'core business', which for the company meant chemicals, not IT. The business units were to be allowed to buy their IT services from the supplier of their choice. If we wanted to survive as an IS organisation, we had to prove our worth to our customers.

The upshot was, we had to get our house in order. We needed to have enough central control to be able to steer the division and maximise the benefits of having a large IS organisation, while allowing each IS unit to be flexible enough to be able to meet local business needs. Our staff had to feel part of one group, with its own identity and mentality. We chose ITIL as our method for getting everyone pulling in the same direction, through the implementation of a Total Quality Programme.

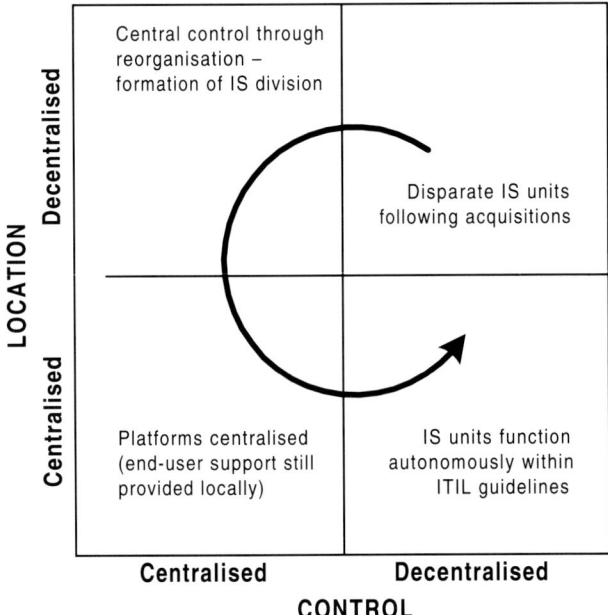

Figure 3.2: Centralised/decentralised IT infrastructure location and control

The IT infrastructure consisted of an amalgam of DEC Vax, IBM 3090, IBM AS400, and Novell networks.

The IS organisation supported the business through provision of manufacturing and office applications.

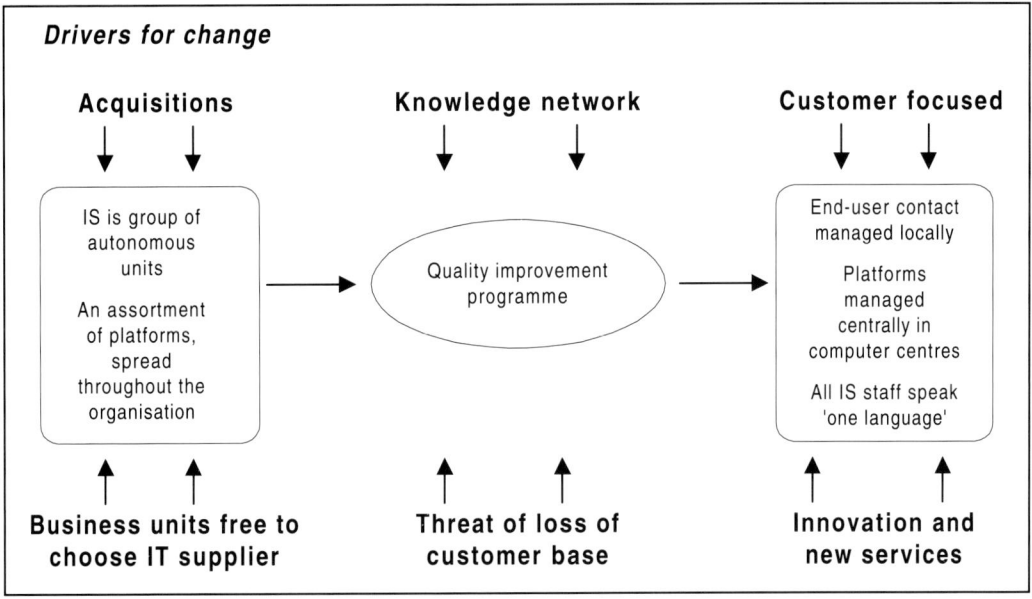

Drivers for change

Figure 3.3: Drivers for change

3.2 Where we wanted to be

A quality improvement programme needs a goal. Without that goal, you lose the motivation of the very people you need to make the programme a success, and you have no chance of achieving the results you want.

We tried to make the improvement programme goals as concrete as we could, and where possible, measurable. We were working with a disparate, international organisation, in which culture, language, customs and even the IS customers were different in each IS unit. We needed to have 'one language' by which everyone could communicate. The language we chose was ITIL

Our principal goal was survival. We had sub-goals by which to achieve this principal goal:

- ensure that all staff speak 'one language'

- ensure an improvement in the customer-perceived quality of IT service provision

- develop clearly defined responsibilities for processes and tasks

- stimulate the development of a 'knowledge network', by which the skills and expertise of our staff could be most effectively used to support our customers.

3.3   How we got there – or not!

The major headache for an IT service provider is balancing the achieved quality of service provision against the level the customer expects. It is an art to get it right!

We started by investigating our customers' expectations and perception of the service levels we were providing. We then objectively examined our service provision capabilities to ensure we were capable of meeting those expectations. The difference between what our customers expected and what we were currently providing, tempered by financial constraints, gave us the scope of the quality improvement programme. In effect, our customers were assisting us in setting our goals and priorities.

Incidentally, we periodically checked with our customers on how we were doing and how we measured up to their expectations. We found that the regular request for feedback was beneficial in developing a healthy working relationship with our customers; we received positive as well as negative criticism, and our customers felt we were taking them seriously.

ITIL – the reference model

We wanted a reference model for the improvement programme, to provide assurance that the goals we had set ourselves were in fact achievable. For the management of IT infrastructure, ITIL was the best available.

The programme was tackled in the form of a structured, but highly fluid project. And we tried to get staff buy-in from the start.

There was no official project leader or rigid project plan: Instead, we had goals, teams, responsibilities, milestones and senior management commitment. We didn't intend to let the project be owned by a single project manager, but by the whole IS organisation!

We involved ten per cent of our staff directly in the programme, who were of all nationalities and experience levels.

We initially tackled the operational level processes, ie the five ITIL service support modules; Help Desk, Problem Management, Change Management, Configuration Management and Software Control and Distribution.

We wanted to establish and improve our work processes so that an employee's actions became process-driven instead of hierarchically driven, for example work activities were to be determined by their place in a process rather than by instructions given by a boss. The overall knowledge and understanding of the work we undertook was to shift down through the organisation to the work floor.

Work groups

Five work groups were established, one per process, each having eight to ten members. The work groups were supported by a steering group, composed of the IT director, an external advisor and the process team managers.

We chose to use a cyclic approach, based on Deming's quality circles. We analysed the current situation, froze it, analysed the bottlenecks and came up with improvements. One improvement level was carried out per cycle, and all processes were improved in parallel.

We went for optimal improvement, which we judged to be overall implementation to 80% of the process according to ITIL, rather than the maximum we could have possibly achieved.

Meetings were forbidden! There is no quicker way to destroy motivation than make people suffer hours of boring meetings. Instead, we instigated work groups, which met once a week under the guidance of an external advisor. There were no minutes, but an action list and a spirit of positive determination which we employed to achieve results. People left the work group sessions pleased with what they had achieved.

The process improvement tasks were fitted in alongside a person's day-to-day work. After all, improving your work is a part of your normal job! Staff responsible for carrying out an activity are often in the best position to say how it can be made more effective or efficient; we gave them the responsibility and authority to carry out the improvement.

If the amount of work was a problem, we hired relief staff to do the 'normal' work and take some of the pressure off our permanent employees.

An incredibly important area of the whole quality programme was public relations, which supported the process work groups. A team of four staff produced weekly newsletters (distributed by e-mail) and posters for office walls.

Folders detailing programme progress were sent to an employee's home address, along with his/her salary slip. This form of mailing was an innovation for our company, and was well-received.

Achieved milestones were celebrated with cake, on which the initials 'ITIL' were iced, and staff were treated to periodic day excursions. We put a lot of effort into creating commitment for the quality improvement programme.

Quick hits

The programme was heavily results-oriented, and geared for results which the customer would notice. We looked for 'quick hits'; anywhere where improvements could be made which quickly showed cost reduction and/or quality improvement. We used existing resources where at all possible in order to keep costs down. No heavy tomes, department manuals or handbooks which could substitute as a doorstop were produced! Instead we developed a quality handbook, process descriptions and supporting procedures to act as a guide for IT service delivery for the distributed IS units. Flowcharts were developed and pinned up on the wall to make the process visible and accessible for everyone.

We developed task-responsibility matrices, so that ownership of activities rested where it belonged.

We needed information on our workload and current performance. How many calls were we handling in a certain time period? Of what priority and impact? How many changes were being requested? We started measuring at the very beginning of the programme and used the information to support decisions as needed.

All IT infrastructure equipment of one type, eg DEC Vax, IBM, was brought together in one physical location for ease of management.

Later in the programme, we established a team of five staff selected from the process work groups to look at potential tools to support the processes.

The whole change process was much slower than expected; we had anticipated that we would achieve our goals within about three months, whereas it took about a year in total. People needed time to get into the swing of the programme, and before we were up to speed we'd had to completely revise our milestones. (But we still had our cake, and ate it!)

3.4   Where we are now

End-user interaction is handled locally at the business unit level. This covers delivery of those IT services required by the end-user, first line support (Help Desk) and handling change requests. This method of working provides maximum flexibility to the customer at the 'point of sale'.

The 'front-end' IT units are supported by the consolidated computer centres and specialist groups, which agree to supply services to the individual units according to specified requirements.

ITIL implementation is considered to be finished to the required maturity level, and to have met its specified goals in supporting the Total Quality Programme. An external auditor was brought in to objectively evaluate the programme, and gave us the 'thumbs-up'!

3.5   Where we go from here

Our next step is to go through the programme again, this time improving our IT service delivery processes. We especially want to improve our service level management process, and develop our customer liaison function. Our intention is to strengthen our relationship with the budget-holding business customers, having already succeeded in improving our relationship with the end-users of our services.

3.6   Lessons learned

If we were about to do the same project again, we wouldn't change a single thing; we are very satisfied with the result. In fact, we are going to follow the same work method for the next programme.

We did, however, learn that you have to watch out for bureaucracy! Try to keep the paperwork to a minimum; go for a balanced approach addressing procedures, people's attitudes, resources and tools, and shared knowledge (synergy in the organisation).

Avoid having meetings, go for work groups instead. And public relations is of the utmost importance! Communicate what you are trying to achieve and how you are approaching it. Try to get early commitment.

We did find that the 'pull' approach, where change was driven by the work groups, demanded a great amount of energy. There is a temptation to lapse into the 'push' approach, where pressure from on-high declares that people either show commitment to the programme, or find themselves another employer! People found it difficult to commit to change, and after all, any change contains a certain amount of pain, until they understood the need for and purpose of the change.

Make the programme goals public, ensure that performance indicators are known, and that progress is communicated to the whole organisation.

Go first for improving the processes which directly affect the end-user, the operational processes and aim for quick, tangible results. And keep your customer involved!

ITIL as an agent for change - study 2

4 ITIL as an agent for change – study 2

*This case study was provided by
The Pink Elephant Group*

4   ITIL as an agent for change – study 2

4.1   Introduction

How would you feel if your local electricity board said they could guarantee to supply you with electricity for 95% of the day? Pleased?

That's one hour and twelve minutes when electricity might not be available. You can bet your cotton socks that in that hour you'd miss your favourite television programme, be gasping for a cup of tea and not even be able to telephone your mother because your cordless 'phone runs off the mains!

In actual fact, figures of 99.99% are more realistic. Electricity boards generally manage their core business well enough to ensure that their customers are provided with their product on demand.

4.2   The starting point

This case describes what happened when an electricity board looked critically at their IT, and realised that 95% availability of IT services was not providing optimal support for the core business.

The utility company in question supplies electricity to a defined geographical region, employing two thousand staff to do so. It has undergone some major changes in the past few years, the principal being a transition from a semi-government institution to an independent company. There have also been some acquisitions of, and fusions and collaborations with, other companies with the aim of being able to purchase bulk quantities of raw materials at a reduced tariff.

The company is composed of four major divisions, responsible for energy distribution, business support activities (eg vehicles, meters) and for the shops, which handle contact with the electricity board customer.

Each division has its own IT unit, which functions independently of the central IS division. The individual IT unit is responsible for its own IT plans, its own purchasing, and its own first-line user support.

The central IS Division provides central IT services, development services, support and attempts to co-ordinate the IS/IT planning through standards and policy.

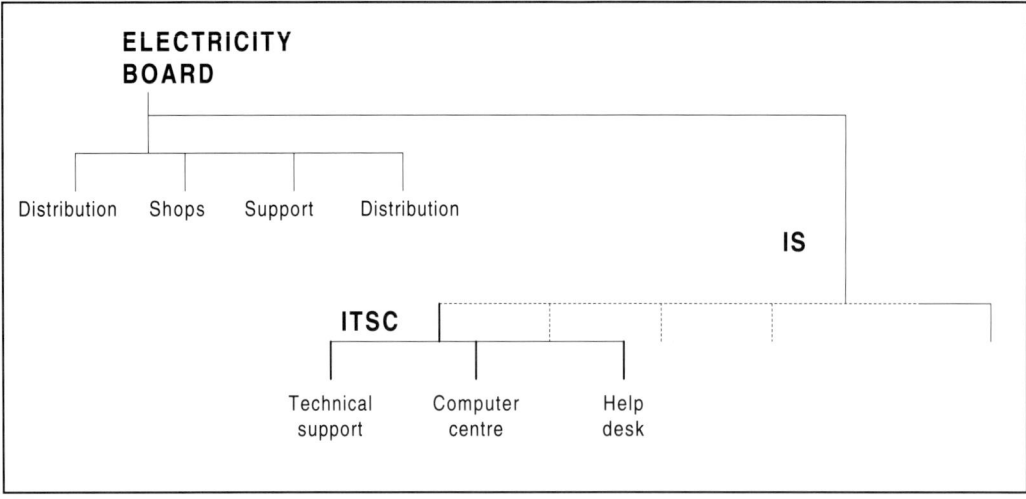

Figure 4.1: Organisation chart

At the start of this quality programme, a department in the IS division which attracted critical review was the IT Service Centre (ITSC).

Senior directors were doubting the need for the organisation to have its own computer centre, and were considering the possibility of outsourcing.

At the same time, there were plans afoot to move to a new application for business support; SAP-RIVA, a package to handle statistics, based on the SAP family of enterprise application systems.

The head of the IS division wanted to know if ITSC was capable of working with the product, as its complexity demands a high-quality IT management organisation. If the answer was 'no ', then ITSC had no added value for the organisation.

He also wanted to know how the IT unit was functioning when compared to other similar IT units. Could the quality of the IT service provision be improved? How satisfied were the end-users with the IT service provision?

There was a major problem which complicated the issue. There was a clash of personalities between the head of IS and the head of the ITSC unit, and they were unable to communicate effectively with each other. This led to poor internal communication, with policy decisions not being passed through to the work floor, and consequent staff demotivation due to lack of direction. Externally, the ITSC was not taken seriously, and had credibility problems in its relationship with end-users.

ITIL consultancy review

Having seen a presentation on ITIL, the head of IS commissioned an ITIL consultancy review of the department. The results confirmed suspicions that the quality of the IT management processes, especially the tactical ones, were currently inadequate to enable introduction of SAP-RIVA.

The investigation also highlighted that inter-departmental communications were poor. IT services were not being delivered to user requirements, and there was considerable dissatisfaction among users, caused by lack of customer contact and lack of information.

Possibly in part due to the friction between departments, it was found that within the ITSC itself, colleagues supported each other, creating a culture in which people and values were considered important. There was little evident respect for regulations or rules, and the department lacked management direction and leadership. Control and structure were considered to be absent, especially when regarded from the end-users' perspective. There was no consultation with the users over longer term IT plans. Innovation, and self-improvement of work, was also conspicuous by its absence. All in all, not a pretty picture!

4.3 The next step

So what was the next step? The IT architecture had been decided on. It was to be based on SAP-RIVA for finance, sales, planning and logistics activities. For company wide support of design work ISICAD was chosen, and PCs were to fulfil the local office systems requirements, providing access to all applications and tools a user needed from his/her own workstation. The network would be based on OS/2 Lan Manager.

The IT services which were to be delivered using these platforms had to meet business requirements, which meant that someone had to talk to the business. The IS division wanted the quality of ITSC IT service delivery to improve. The IT service management processes were to be brought to a maturity level which demonstrated that ITSC had control over its processes, with clearly defined tasks and responsibilities, standards, a modular handbook and with procedures and guidelines being developed to support the provision of IT services.

4.4   How they did it

A quality improvement programme was set up in the form of a project. The review had covered the IT processes service level management, configuration management, Help Desk, problem management, change management, availability management and cost management. These processes would be improved over the following year and another review would check on progress at the end of the project.

There followed a two month phase in which relevant information was gathered and consultations were held with representatives of the business, which led to the development of a project plan.

From the information gathering, it was clear that the following was needed:

- a clearly communicated mission statement

- an unequivocal organisational structure

- clearly communicated task responsibilities

- formal reporting and communication lines

- a split between IT support and production

- eradication of unnecessary tasks.

It was obvious that communication and clarity of purpose were areas which needed some attention.

Major problems

At the start of the project it was possible to identify some major problems, which may be inherent in a 'public service' organisation. Work tended to be divided up on the basis of status, 'empires' and personal preferences, rather than looking at the underlying processes driving the work. This meant that the divisions of labour were not always the most efficient or effective for the work which had to be done, and led to islands being formed which had their own personalised goalsets, often conflicting with those of the organisation as a whole.

Despite recognition that the recommendations from the IT service management review needed to be implemented, no one in ITSC really believed they would work. The department was suffering from 'Consultitis', (a surfeit of consultancy), and a lack of belief in its abilities. Management displayed no motivation for staff management, with the result that the staff had little motivation for the work.

There was no formal (or even informal) structure for communication and reporting, which exacerbated the general feeling of helplessness and hopelessness on the part of the staff.

Interdepartmental co-ordination had not been well managed. The fact that each business division had its own IT unit and could buy its own IT equipment meant that configuration management was a nightmare! (The configuration database was, in fact, found to be full of rubbish data. It was decided not to clean it, but to move to a new system and enter the correct data from scratch.)

ITSC was functioning as a second-line support unit without agreeing responsibilities and aligning expectations with the first-line unit. Agreeing a service level agreement with users in this sort of situation is almost impossible.

The project plan was divided into two phases.

Phase one

Phase one clearly defined the scope of the project within the organisation. The activities included:

- creation of a mission statement

- definition of services, and production of a service catalogue which contains a list of the IT services, categorised into priority groups

- identification of tasks and responsibilities

- documentation of user requirements, and hence derivation of service level requirements

- definition of a communication model for the project, and for the organisation when the project is complete.

It was recommended that IS be reorganised, so that the number of IT units was reduced to four. ITSC was abolished. Instead, a User Support Centre and a Computer Centre were created.

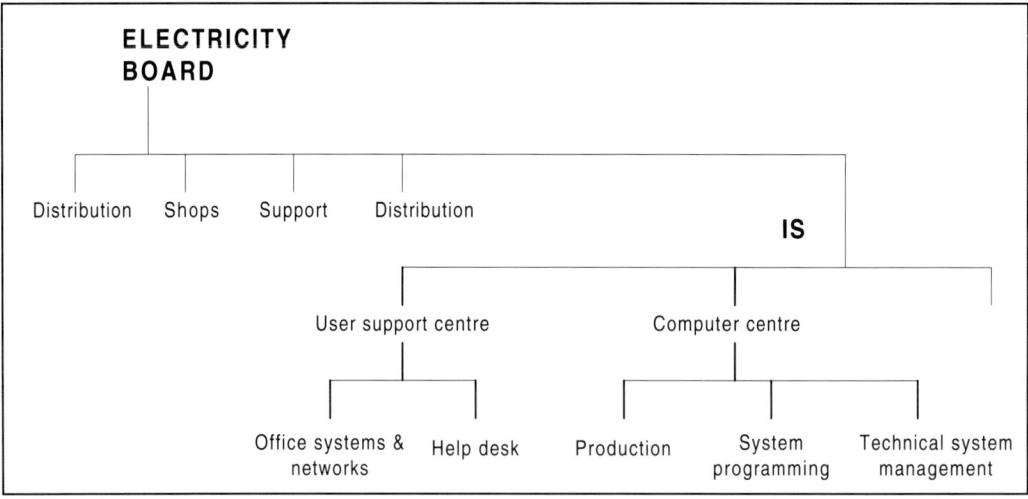

Figure 4.2: New organisation

The Computer Centre covered only mainframes and contained the sub-units of System Programming, Production and Technical System management. Its principal function was to provide cost effective services for the user applications and IT infrastructure, that is, facility management and support.

The User Support Unit contained the sub-units Help Desk, and Office Systems and Networks. Its core tasks were to identify, solve and prevent incidents in IT service delivery and to manage the organisation's network facilities.

Communication

A formal communication structure was proposed for the IT units:

- a daily morning work discussion in which unsolved incidents and problems were examined

- a weekly problem meeting, in which longer term problems were examined, and action taken to clear them

- a weekly change meeting, (in fact a Change Advisory Board meeting), in which proposed changes were examined, and decisions taken on whether/when to implement them

- a fortnightly general planning and personnel meeting

- a monthly (internal) service level meeting in which the general performance of the IT unit was examined

- a monthly (external) service level meeting in which the customer took part.

Phase two

Phase two covered the implementation of ITIL processes. Critical success factors were identified as:

- the proposed organisational change being implemented according to the phase one proposal

- commitment to the project being actively demonstrated by management

- no moving goalposts

- a quality programme (including training) for all staff

- adequate resources (ie people).

The staff active in the project were grouped into teams, each of which had a particular role. With hindsight, the project structure was mimicking the hierarchical culture of the organisation itself, and took the problems inherent in the organisation with it. Another structure would have been more appropriate, for example, having line management lead the implementation instead of using a formal project structure.

Nevertheless, the project structure comprised three layers and was headed by a sponsoring senior manager, the head of IS.

The layers were made up of a steering group, who acted as a source of advice for the project, a project group, who co-ordinated the activities of the work groups, and three work groups, each led by a manager who was in turn a member of the project group. The work groups were split into areas of responsibility:

- problem management, Help Desk and configuration management

- change management

- service level management, cost management and availability management.

The plan for phase two was composed of a series of general steps:

- form the project steering, project and work groups
- ITIL training, to get everyone thinking along the same lines
- project training
- set up handbook
- set up procedures, standards and guidelines

which were in turn supplemented by workgroup-specific activities. As an example 'Plan and Implement Help Desk Improvement':

- appoint a Help Desk supervisor
- define role Help Desk
- record current working practices
- categorise incidents
- define relationships with other processes and departments
- write procedures
- record tools available
- specify metrics
- improve accommodation
- decide on communication to users
- decide on management reporting
- decide on audits
- write implementation plan
- implement.

The Help Desk was implemented in the form of one central desk which staff units could call directly and four distributed Help Desks for support of the business units. The Help Desk staff were given formal training and were coached by allocating experienced staff to educate those with less experience. Secondments to the computer centre were organised. The aim was to clear 80% of calls at the Help Desk, without referral to second-line support. The task was clear and staff were enthusiastic.

Implementation problems

During phase two, an audit took place to look at the implementation problems. It was found that two projects were having a major impact on the quality improvement programme. These projects, conversion of a mainframe operating system, and the move to SAP-RIVA, were both allocated a higher priority in management attention. There was too little management commitment and no actual hands-on steering. The amount of resources actually available for the ITIL implementation was well below that required and requested at the outset. The project was hindered by bureaucracy and hierarchy.

The knowledge and capabilities of the IT unit staff were found to be below the expected and required level. For example, it necessitated the introduction of the coaching scheme for Help Desk staff.

There was a natural aversion to change, and an unwillingness to undertake any actions to change. This was typified by the fact that one appointed member of the steering group never showed up for a meeting.

Not enough attention was given to the steering group at the beginning of the project. They hadn't been through ITIL training and often either forgot or didn't understand their role. If a work group produced a piece of work, such as a procedure or plan, the steering group would often have a different interpretation of its content to that intended by the work group and would devote much of its energy to discussions concerning content.

It was also shown that problems with particular members of staff, who were deliberately obstructing implementation of ITIL, were circumvented. Senior management did not want to take on a confrontation. Ninety per cent of problems in the project were political.

Improvements

However, despite these problems during the project, there was a change of staff mentality. People began to work proactively, producing ideas to improve their work. Customer and service orientation was clearly improved, aided by increased staff awareness of the goals and functions of the IS division. This all helped to increase the knowledge, motivation and involvement of staff.

The reorganisation was declared a success, while ITIL provided an insight into the IT costs, and enabled a charging structure to be put in place.

For the Computer Centre, ITIL meant that:

- tasks were defined

- reports were improved, and contained meaningful information

- a daily meeting was established, which assisted in improving communication

- production planning was implemented.

For the User Support Centre (Office Systems), ITIL meant that:

- a renewed configuration management was established

- problem management was greatly improved

- all changes to the IT infrastructure passed through the change management process

- incident control has gained recognition as being of crucial importance for the business customer

- a daily meeting was established, which assisted in improving communication

- reports were improved, and contained meaningful information

- central and distributed Help Desks have been established.

Staff have benefited in terms of experience and their career opportunities.

4.5   Where they are now

Areas which still need addressing include customer contact. Users are still not receiving the operational and tactical level information they require.

Procedures have been drawn up, but they have not resulted in an improvement in the perceived quality of the IT services by the customer. Efficiency improvements are mainly in the operational level processes, and have not yet been implemented in the tactical level processes, where the customer experiences the benefit.

The procedures are inward looking and do not really consider the customer's or a peer department's perspective. The procedures also exceed the original scope of the project, and require the co-operation of other departments to make them function correctly. It was also noted that staff do not necessarily follow the procedures in their day-to-day work!

The project 'Quality improvement through ITIL implementation' has led to the customer having increased expectations of the IT unit, which cannot all be fulfilled at present.

A review of the processes after implementation showed that problem management and the Help Desk function were formalised, with management reports, definition of tasks and authorisation, documentation of procedures, work instructions and planning all having been defined and implemented. The change management, configuration management, availability management and cost management processes were found still to have shortcomings, in that the quality of management reports were not yet up to standard and the processes did not function as described in the documented work instructions and procedures. Service level management was still in its infancy.

4.6	Where next?

The next step is to complete the implementation of and consolidate these processes, and to begin implementation of tactical level processes. A major area still to be addressed is the relationship with the customer, preferably to be formalised through the use of negotiated service level agreements. The customer requirements can be translated into operational targets for the IT organisation, and assist in steering the work of the unit.

4.7	Conclusion

If the project was being tackled again, it would probably be done in a much less structured way. The method of formally documenting everything before implementation increased bureaucracy and produced no 'quick hits' to assist in motivation and direction forming within the project. People had the impression that all the effort put into the project was merely producing a pile of paper!

Implementing a systems managed environment

5   Implementing a systems managed environment

*This case study was provided by
F.I. Group plc*

5 Implementing a systems managed environment

5.1 Introduction

This case study looks at the ITIL issues that arose when a medium-sized company in the financial and pensions sector, was acquired by a larger company with similar interests. The smaller company's IT department dealt with independent PC-based applications together with local UNIX and other mini-based systems. The Applications Support Teams supported over fourteen major systems spread over forty offices nation-wide.

A reorganisation took place after the acquisition to provide a stronger focus on service delivery. There was pressure to introduce ITIL best practices from the mainframe-orientated acquiring company.

The case study looks at the pragmatic approach taken to implementing ITIL procedures appropriate to PC- and LAN-based systems. It highlights the danger of underestimating the effort and tools required to implement ITIL modules and shows what can be achieved even with these constraints.

5.2 Where we were

Configuration Management	There was an existing asset register, but the validity of the information on this was felt to be doubtful, and it was updated only twice a year.
Help Desk	Originally incidents were dealt with by the individual support teams, with users ringing the support teams directly with their problems. There had been a Help Desk for PC support that had worked well.
Support groups	In addition, there were local operations and support groups spread around the country that dealt with basic hardware problems, and acted as a filter for common easy-to-solve incidents.
Problem Management	The only problem management in operation was an unofficial analysis undertaken within the support teams. Some teams had a paper Known Error list and one of the Help Desk staff who had previously been on support also had a card index file with common errors that had come to her attention.
Change Management	Some systems already had change procedures in place, but these were not consistent, and some areas had no procedures at all.

	Service Level Agreements (SLAs)	Due to previous reorganisations and take-overs of small firms, no one had an overall view of all the systems the Applications Support team were supporting, and there were no formal Service Level Agreements (SLAs) or definitions.
	Availability Management	Some information was available on types of hardware, but this had not been considered in conjunction with availability of the systems themselves.
5.3	**Where we wanted to be**	As part of the management reorganisation there was a process review of the Operational Services section, which decided to introduce Systems Management principles into the organisation. A two day Systems Management Workshop was therefore held with the objectives of:

- agreeing a mission statement

- defining and prioritising action plans to achieve the mission

- establishing a team with commitment to the agreed activities.

As part of the workshop there was a brainstorming session on critical success factors and a review of the effectiveness of the current processes within the Operational Services Department. These were then used to develop action plans and initiate a number of projects, including:

- providing an integrated Help Desk

- change management

- problem management

- availability management

- defining the roles and responsibilities of local and regional support

- staff

- instituting SLAs.

The agreed mission statement was as follows:

To implement a systems managed environment for the provision of the company's computer facilities in the UK, to measured levels of service, by June 1994.

5.4   How we got there

Although the target date gave a timescale of three months, only the Help Desk project was assigned to a member of staff without other commitments. As a result only the integrated Help Desk was operational by the target date.

A Service Manager was appointed at this time to continue with the ITIL initiatives already started, and an external consultant was contracted to work with her to review the Help Desk and to assist in drafting roles and responsibilities and procedures.

Their first task was to decide which was the order of priority for the implementation of the ITIL Service Delivery elements. They initiated the following projects, with priority being given to change management:

- inventory control as a first step to configuration management

- problem management

- change management

- training in ITIL concepts

- availability management

- roles, responsibilities and scope of local support groups

- service definition, and production of a skeleton SLA in preparation for SLA negotiation

- introduction of new Help Desk software that would also integrate problem and change management.

Configuration Management

During the Service Workshop the management team had originally given Configuration Management a lower priority, because it was seen to be too difficult to implement at the same time as a parallel Office Automation project was taking place.

However, the newly appointed Service Manager, with the consultant, decided that the planned roll out of Office Automation (OA) was an ideal opportunity to gather information on the hardware in place within the company.

They felt that to institute full Configuration Management, ie both version control of all configurable items and the relationship between them, without appropriate tools being in place, and with all the other changes occurring, would be too resource intensive. Therefore, a project should be initialised looking at Inventory Management of configurable items but not attempting to map the relationships between them.

Help Desk

A Help Desk Manager was appointed who had been a team leader for one of the major systems, and Help Desk software was developed in-house using the PC-based Q&A database manager package.

The Help Desk was based on the 'intelligent model' with the Help Desk staff having a mixture of skills including business knowledge, plus systems knowledge with good PC and word processing skills.

The external consultant's review was carried out after the Help Desk had been in operation for three months. This review found that, despite the lack of resources and the limited Help Desk software, the procedures had worked well, with all calls being routed to the Help Desk.

As a result the Help Desk was working efficiently as an incident logging point and managing to clear around 50% of incidents without referring to second-line support. However, it was reactive rather than proactive as there were no problem management procedures in place and no priority codes or target response times were set.

It became obvious that a more flexible support tool was required, which would integrate incident control and problem and change management and provide a Known Error database, preferably linking from the start to an Inventory system and eventually to a full configuration management database.

Initially Help Desk Exec was the preferred tool of the Help Desk Manager although it did not fully meet the Groups' needs. Eventually it was decided to investigate IHD (IBM's Integrated Help Desk).

Problem Management

The priority was to load errors and problems into a Known Error database, appoint a Problem Manager with responsibility for analysing incidents to identify underlying causes and to agree priority and severity codes, plus target response times.

The procedures for problem management were drafted, but it was decided to delay implementation of them until the new Help Desk software was installed, as the Q&A database did not easily allow for prioritisation of calls, nor provide a sufficiently speedy look-up on other databases such as a Known Error database.

Change Management

It was decided that change management should have a high priority and could be tackled without problem management being in operation and could, if necessary, be a paper-based system and not, therefore, dependant on the new Help Desk software.

Procedures were written which outlined the roles and responsibilities of the Change Manager, Change Co-ordinator, Change Requestor, Change Implementor and Change Builder. A request for change (RFC) form was designed, with an RFC log, and it was decided that these procedures should be followed both in Application Support and also in Operations.

As the Group procedures specified that any changes over ten man/days have to be lodged as a project and follow project procedures, it was decided that the need for a Change Advisory Board for changes outside the authorisation limits of the Change Manager was not necessary.

A great deal of discussion took place with the teams, who were initially reluctant to accept that small changes of under one man-day should go through this procedure. Some ITIL training was undertaken, which raised awareness of the importance of including all effort, testing and implementing in the estimate. As a result the teams agreed that all changes, no matter how minor, should go through the change procedure.

The procedures were piloted in the two areas perceived to be most problematic, PC support and PC movement. This gave rise to a number of amendments in the RFC form. Unfortunately, the volume of changes in these areas was low and did not constitute a representative pilot. When the procedures were extended to other areas, it became apparent that a paper-based system was too time consuming, and the RFC form and log were transferred on to a Q&A database.

Service Level Agreements (SLAs)	The Service Manager together with the consultant undertook a comprehensive Service Level Definition review. Once this had been completed a skeleton SLA was drawn up.
Availability Management	A metrics gathering exercise on the availability record of different types of hardware was undertaken, however, without a more appropriate Help Desk tool, it was not possible to measure the overall availability of software.

5.5 Where we are now

Configuration Management	The detail to be held for both hardware and software, has now been defined and is awaiting the appropriate tool to be put into action.
	Meanwhile a simplified inventory database has been created with a record of all users and their software. This is being compiled during the Office Automation (OA) roll out and input into a Hardcat asset register. Ultimately it will be used to populate the new Help Desk and Configuration Management tool.
Help Desk	The decision has not yet been reached on an integrated Help Desk tool. Therefore, some further tailoring of the Q&A database has been undertaken which, although not ideal, is proving to be a reasonable stop-gap. The Help Desk staff have had ITIL awareness training and are providing a good centralised service to the users.
	The Help Desk has increased the number of incidents resolved by them, and has built up a good reputation with the users. The consequential reduction in the volume of calls going to second-line support has reduced the number of staff required in applications support and hence the overall cost.
Problem Management	Some Problem Management has been achieved even without a PMS system, and in one particular area studying the underlying causes of the problems has halved the number of calls. Identification of trends has started, and the Help Desk staff are more aware of the problem management issues rather than simply being concerned with 'fire-fighting'. As a result the resolution rate by the Help Desk has increased from 40% to 50%.
	Problem management techniques were used when the number of incidents on the OA roll out started to escalate, and this was of considerable benefit in

highlighting to the third party supplier the underlying problems causing the incidents.

It would have been beneficial, with hindsight, to have implemented an interim tool solution to problem management. It was assumed that the new Help Desk software would have been procured more quickly and, therefore, that it was a waste of resources to tailor the existing system. If this had been done, metrics gathering on priority of calls could have been started earlier, more trends identified, and a basic Known Error database installed.

Change Management

A specification for a medium-term solution is now underway as the Q&A database has a number of shortcomings.

Generally change management procedures have made staff far more aware of the need for accurate reporting and estimating. In Operations, measurable targets have been set against number of changes implemented.

Until an integrated tool is available a Lotus Notes Database will be used. This will allow different views of the change request form depending upon what type of change is underway. For example, the Operations section found it time consuming to use a RFC that was designed for both Software and Hardware.

Service Level Agreements

The Service Manager has met with the service owners and has issued the skeleton SLA to the main business areas, feedback from the users has been positive so far.

As problem management procedures have not been implemented with the priority levels the metrics have not yet been gathered. It is felt that it will be necessary to record these for three months before agreeing a baseline.

Availability Management

More information has been gained on what the primary components of the systems are, and which are the service stoppers. There is now a heightened awareness of the importance of availability management and the impact that this area has on SLAs.

5.6   General issues and lessons learned

Overall the exercise has been beneficial, even in those areas of service delivery that do not yet have a fully operational procedure.

The timescale needed to put procedures into place was underestimated at first. The exercise is both time consuming and resource intensive.

A major factor in delaying the start of projects was how little time people had available. The projects moved ahead much more quickly once a dedicated Service Manager was in place.

The decision to wait for the introduction of a specific integrated Help Desk tool that would include change, problem and configuration management was, in retrospect, incorrect. An interim solution should have been sought while the decisions about tools were being made. However, no one anticipated the extra time that the interface with the new Group management would take.

It is expected that when an integrated Help Desk and problem and change management tool with a Known Error database is in place the resolution of calls by the Help Desk will increase to around 70%.

Key lessons

In summary the key lessons learnt were as follows:

- ensure that agreement is forthcoming to release staff to devote to ITIL initiatives

- ensure that tactical as well as strategic plans are incorporated into the schedule so that movement can be on several fronts at once

- always look at the process as a whole as well as looking at the individual projects.

Benefits

General benefits have been:

- a reduction in resources needed for applications support

- a reduction in volume of incidents coming through to the Help Desk

- an increased resolution of incidents at the Help Desk level

- increased awareness of the importance of SLAs especially when dealing with third party support.

The aim is to continue with the ITIL initiatives already started, implementing where necessary medium term software solutions, so that some of the initiatives can move ahead without the new Help Desk software being in place.

Delivering an application support and maintenance service

6 Delivering an application support and maintenance service

*This case study was provided by
FI Group plc*

6 Delivering an application support and maintenance service

6.1 Introduction	F.I. Group plc (FI) has been a supplier of third party application support and maintenance for a number of years. When the ITIL Library became available FI trained its Application Support consultants and Service Managers in ITIL Service Support and Service Delivery and reviewed its Application Support service against the relevant ITIL functions. This was to ensure that the service followed recognised standards and to provide a means of continually improving the effectiveness and efficiency of the service provided.
	This approach is illustrated by looking at how FI delivers an Application Support service for a range of customers across a variety of platforms applying the most relevant ITIL Service Support and Service Delivery elements. All the techniques described are equally applicable to providing an in-house software support service.
	The case study starts by describing what FI finds in terms of the ITIL Service Support and Service Delivery elements at the beginning of a project with a new customer. It then goes on to describe how we apply ITIL best practices to the service and what benefits this approach provides. It ends by looking at the expected future direction of Application Support services and the likely relevance of ITIL.
6.2 Where we start from	Although each organisation is unique in its approach to software support we find that they have a lot in common and the findings listed below are typical across the range of organisations which we service.
ITIL Service Support elements	Hardly any organisations have a fully comprehensive centralised Configuration Management Database, covering hardware, software and data.
	It is rare for organisations to make a clear distinction between incidents, problems and known errors. They do not collect and report useful metrics and therefore do not have an adequate Problem Management System.
	Most mature IT departments have formal change management along ITIL lines for large enhancements

and developments but not for smaller, maintenance-type changes.

It is usual to find a central, non-expert IT Help Desk using a tool for logging incidents, but often it is difficult to ensure that all application incidents are logged via the Help Desk.

Virtually all our customers have formal software control and distribution mechanisms and authorisation procedures, with some release planning and some contingency/regression planning.

ITIL Service Delivery elements

It is usual to find Service Level Agreements (SLAs) between operations and user areas defining the on-line service hours, percentage availability and sometimes system response times and critical deadlines but extremely rare to find an SLA specifically covering application support.

Organisations tend to have basic capacity management covering disk capacity and data storage only.

The majority of our customers have contingency planning, controlled security and access (sometimes less well controlled for PCs) and some formal risk assessment identifying critical systems and critical times.

We rarely find formal availability management for application software. Optimisation of software availability relies almost exclusively on the experience and skill of the support teams.

The majority of our customers do not have formal cost management of their Support and Maintenance function and this may be a major factor in the decision to outsource application support.

6.3 Where we want to be

FI's key objectives for the application support covering both Service Support and Service Delivery are:

- deliver the contracted service reliably and efficiently

- enhance the systems' performance and availability through cost effective preventive maintenance

- provide a more cost effective service by increasing the productivity of the support team.

6.4   How we get there

The Application Support service is tailored to function within each customer environment, using existing formal procedures and tools, and normally operating as a specialist support group within the customer's IT department.

The areas where we deliver most benefit are those directly or partially under our control and these are the ones described below.

6.4.1   ITIL Service Support Elements

Configuration Management

As a first step in Configuration Management, we document the installation naming conventions. We then produce a 'configuration map' of the environment(s), menus, libraries, system, application software and documentation.

Code movement is controlled by library management tools with cross reference to configuration items (CIs) where appropriate. For example, in one case, CIs already under development were identified, showing location, status and ownership by application, change or problem number. Entries were archived after implementation to form a change history.

We instigate version numbering if this is not already in place, and maintain an amendment history, including the description, date, owner, change, problem, release, amendment and version number as comments at the start of each CI entry.

Problem Management

Our approach to problem management is based on ensuring that all problems have an owner, that initial emphasis is on system recovery and incident resolution, and that relevant metrics are collected to ensure timely and targeted problem identification.

We identify a Problem Manager (often on a team rota basis) who manages all problems associated with the systems under our care, whether they are caused by application software or something else (eg hardware, network, operations or user instructions).

We concentrate on fast response diagnosis and system recovery, making the system available for use as soon as possible. This action is then followed up by full impact analysis, problem resolution and cost-justified preventive maintenance.

We identify performance indicators for the agreed service and collect relevant metrics so that we can report against these to identify trends and monitor service delivery performance. The metrics will be tailored to the needs of each organisation but typically include:

- responsiveness and effectiveness of the service (time to respond, fix by priority)

- weak components

- accuracy of changes

- numbers of incidents/problems over time by priority downtime

- support effort – normal and 'out-of-hours'.

Change Management

The discipline of having a contractual agreement for support and maintenance drives organisations towards more formal change management. Changes are identified as Work Parcels within the contract and are sized, costed and formally signed off by the customer's Change Manager/Contract Manager.

FI's approach is formal. We review and prioritise any backlog of change requests with the customer at the start of the project and at regular intervals thereafter. We then log change requests and provide timely estimates of impact and effort to the customer so that he can assess the cost/benefit and agree priorities. Finally we bundle approved change requests, where possible within priorities and timescales, for cost-effective development/testing.

Applying formal change procedures to all outstanding requests can have dramatic results. For one customer we were able to reduce a three year backlog to less than two months for high priority changes by agreeing with users what was essential, applying cost benefit analysis to all changes and removing cosmetic change requests.

6.4.2 ITIL Service Delivery elements

Service Level Management

As well as complying with any existing SLAs FI expects to work to a formal SLA. The focus is on delivering benefits to the business both in terms of the application (its functionality and deliverables), and the Application Management Service itself. We proactively monitor the regular business critical deliverables (reports, transmissions, interface dependencies, on-line availability).

FI works closely with the users to 'fine-tune' both the application and the service in response to specific business needs. Typically these include:

- ensuring availability at business critical times

- tuning performance and throughput at peak times such as year end

- planning or rescheduling for unusual business periods (eg holidays)

- providing additional or improved functionality.

Targets for the service are defined in conjunction with the business, and the service is monitored and regularly reviewed for key performance indicators including responsiveness, productivity, accuracy and quality. We frequently find that there are unstated requirements in the service required. In one case the delivery of a weekly sales report to the directors had the highest possible priority although this was not specified anywhere. As a result we built this into our own service definition although it never became part of the formal SLA.

Capacity Management

Capacity management is addressed both directly and indirectly. We estimate capacity and performance impact of software changes as part of change management and estimate peak load requirements as part of risk management.

We identify, via the problem management system, capacity or performance issues that require increasing capacity or database reorganisation or clear-down. We give the support team guidelines for optimising performance and storage utilisation and ensure that the guidelines are followed.

Availability Management

Availability relies heavily on good change and problem management. Effective service reporting metrics, collected via the problem management mechanism, are essential to identify trends, vulnerabilities and threats to availability.

FI aims to improve application reliability by reducing the overall number of incidents occurring, particularly those involving downtime, by cost-justified preventive maintenance. This may cover a number of vulnerable system components including storage utilisation, database and file organisation, user instructions and training, operator instructions and training, documentation and system interfaces. Reliability is also improved by better quality control, testing and implementation procedures for both application and system changes.

Availability can be improved significantly by preventive maintenance on batch operations. One of our customers had a very tight batch window where one failure in the run could delay the start of the on-line service by over two hours. We created intermediate back-up and recovery points in the batch run reducing the recovery time to ten minutes and eliminating the need to repeat the whole batch run in the event of the failure.

Cost Management

The very fact of outsourcing, and transfer of 'real' money tends to crystallise the cost issue, since a charging mechanism must be in place. Formalised change management results in improved cost management and better control of how resources are utilised and money spent.

Cost effectiveness and productivity are carefully monitored, comparing actuals against estimates. The scope and cost of the support service is periodically renegotiated so that the service continues to meet changing business needs and remains cost effective.

6.5 Benefits of applying ITIL principles

The benefits derived from applying the best practices of the various ITIL elements tend to overlap but for clarity they are listed by element below.

Configuration Management

Consistent, reliable impact analysis which facilitates change and problem diagnosis and reduces risk.

Less reliance on the knowledge of key individuals and better cross-skilling within the support team improving flexibility and productivity.

Tighter control of the systems portfolio, reducing errors at all stages of the maintenance process.

Problem Management

Improved productivity and system availability.

Improved user confidence – problems are satisfactorily resolved, and the business kept informed.

Better control with a measured, improving service.

	Change Management	The customer can make more effective decisions based on the known cost and benefits of requested changes.
		Better control and planning – changes delivered are accurate and within known timescales, enabling both the IT department and users to plan ahead.
		Increased productivity for the IT department and users.
	Service Level Management	Application Management service and application deliverables tuned to business needs.
	Availability Management	Improved application reliability, maintainability and expected life span.
		Risk identification and reduction.
	Cost Management	Containment of cost and targeted control of IT budget.
6.5.1	Overall ITIL Service Support and Delivery benefits	Demonstrable productivity gains of 20% to 50%.
		Reduction or elimination of IT management effort spent 'fire fighting'.
		Improved flexibility and responsiveness to business needs.
		Improved user perception and confidence from a professional relationship with users.

6.6 Where we want to go in the future

FI consistently finds that outsourcing of the Support and Maintenance function tends to formalise the application management process and drive organisations towards ITIL best practices. The more that ITIL practices are followed by an organisation the easier it is to implement a cost effective, high quality, Application Support service.

From FI's viewpoint the incorporation of ITIL best practices is a key factor in the process of continually refining our Application Support service to increase the benefits and provide value for money. We work in partnership with our customers to improve the cost effectiveness of the Application Support service within the overall service framework supplied by our customers to their users.

Increasingly, FI is being asked to provide the same quality of service in distributed or client/server applications with their more complex series of interactive technologies. Typically in these environments many of the mainframe ITIL best practices have not been implemented. We are convinced that it is essential that ITIL principles be applied in this arena if the promised business benefits and improved responsiveness of client/server developments are to be delivered.

Technological change, market testing and agency status

7 Technological change, market testing and agency status

This case study was provided by
The Quint Wellington Redwood Group

7 Technological change, market testing and agency status

> *'What is the use of a book', thought Alice,*
> *'without pictures or conversations?'*
> Lewis Carroll

This is a case study about a government department IT Directorate and the way in which it approached, in Service Management terms, technological change, market testing and agency status. ITIL formed the basis of that approach but there was more to it, so much more, than could be read in the books.

7.1 Where were we?

By the autumn of 1990, the departmental IT strategy was set and it had become clear that, despite a wholesale move towards UNIX and client/server computing for much of the newly planned application software development, the mainframe processes would be required for a number of years yet. So, how could that situation be managed to ensure that:

- ♥ each existing mainframe system had a suitable configuration on which to run for the rest of its life?

- ♥ the quality, reliability and availability of IT services was improved?

- ♥ the costs of providing services were lowered?

  (And why didn't we think of flexibility, I wonder, because it became one of the most significant factors.)

The answer to the first and third objectives lay in restructuring the existing mainframe sites and resources so that significant overhead and staff savings could be made in their operation and management. In total there were 298 staff involved in providing IT services, excluding applications development and general administration and planning. How the reduction was more than achieved within a fairly short period of time does not form part of this detailed case study, but the fact that it provided a hook upon which to hang – and justify – the second objective was crucial to the success of the whole exercise. And there were some lessons to be learned:

- ♣ mammoth IS consultancy studies have a habit of producing mammoth amounts of paper and looking, *in far too much detail*, too far forward. If you build upon their detail, you are building upon sand. And further, they tend to repeat themselves endlessly. This is a technique used by all project managers to instil belief in the veracity of what they say and write!

  'What I tell you three times is true.'

- ♣ to gain general acceptance of where, in broad terms, you think you want to go is important; to plan the framework that should take you there is extremely important; to know what the next step should be is crucial; to know where to begin is vital. So …

  'Begin at the beginning,' the King said, gravely, 'and go on till you come to the end: then stop.'

7.2 How, exactly, did we start?	Activities had actually started a little earlier in that year. That was when the concept of having Service Level Agreements had been widely discussed – and indeed the idea of them had become fashionable throughout government IT circles. Here, then, was the second hook, for the Service Level Manager post established to negotiate and conclude these agreements was to provide just the additional resource we required in order to make progress on that second objective.

By June 1991, therefore, we had completed the study into the future management of our IT Services infrastructure. Why did there have to be a formal 'study'? Simply because that was what the book said we had to do. And, for all its fine words, did it convince one single soul outside of the project of the sense of our objectives, of the urgent need to change? I doubt it! Indeed, its thoroughness (indigestibility?) may have made it seem even more suspect – for by now the opposition was beginning to awake and it is entirely natural to suspect what you do not understand.

And the fact that you have enthusiasts in your midst …

Why, sometimes I've believed as many as six impossible things before breakfast.

… makes the situation even more suspicious.

Objectives

The objectives of our study were to:

♦ identify the most suitable approach to the implementation of the principles of the CCTA IT Infrastructure Library within the directorate's IT Services division

(How carefully we had avoided suggesting that the project might stray into other areas of the directorate! A nonsense of course since, as became quite clear later on, any project of this nature must encompass the whole of the IS management activity in order to be successful.)

♦ prepare cost and resource estimates for full implementation of the recommended approach and plan in detail the next phase

(Note that we did not have to promise to make savings of any particular magnitude since our first 'hook' had provided all the financial justification needed. However, that did not absolve us from attempting an estimate of the benefits – see later.)

Scope

In addition to the above, the scope of the project was set out in detail. This was to:

♠ examine current IT service management procedures and establish appropriate metrics in order to set a baseline and to identify those areas which will obtain most benefit from implementing ITIL disciplines

(A very good place to start. But be careful how you criticise current practices and procedures for it is not the management of today's services that you are concerned with, it is whether today's methods will be suitable for tomorrow's services.)

♠ review available software tools for IT infrastructure management. Assess the extent to which requirements are (or will be) satisfied by such tools

(A necessary activity but, as the second item in the list, it was in the wrong place. Having come to realise that, whatever the departmental pressures, Service Level Agreements were almost the last things we should be concerned with at this stage, we were also beginning to understand that a software-led project was not a sensible way to proceed. Before tools are bought there needs to be a detailed understanding of how they are going to be used – and by whom! We were not at that stage. Still, it did no harm to look.)

♠ produce an outline implementation plan for ITIL – to reflect an objective assessment of priorities as well as logical dependencies

(We knew that there would be insufficient resources to progress at a common speed on a broad front. So we had to decide what fitted best with what and where the greatest paybacks were.)

♠ structure the plan into logical stages that can be progressed with a high degree of independence, according to resource availability; the plan to contain details of effort, skills, timescales and costs (including software and hardware)

(We were beginning to understand that, just as the May 1991 BCS Release 2 Industry Structure Model had predicted, a host of different skills are needed to manage a modern IS infrastructure and that it was important to start sorting out the differently shaped pegs, partly through trial and error, partly through training.)

The rule is, jam tomorrow and jam yesterday –
but never jam today.

♠ produce a cost estimate for each stage and identify the expected benefits, tangible and otherwise.

(In the event, and probably in common with most other projects of this nature, no singular cost saving attributable directly to infrastructure management changes was ever identified. The direct savings arising from, for example, the greater automation of operations management could be and were estimated at this stage. However, the statistics needed to estimate the measurable savings later achieved from (say) a reduction in the numbers of failures attributable to service changes were simply not there.)

7.3 The opposition

The result of all this activity was that those intimately involved became resolutely convinced of the sense of the ITIL approach to service management. However, those around them – including some at the highest levels of management in the directorate – remained sceptical or, at best, supportive but unconvinced that radical change would be required in order to survive. In the end, it was not so much the lack of direct support that mattered, but the variable nature of that support.

Will you, won't you, will you, won't you, will you join the dance?

But who can blame them?

If everyone minded their own business ... the world would go round a deal faster than it does.

As in many IT organisations, each 'division' had its own agenda, felt its own threats, and had developed its own set of relationships. Each resisted change unless it had been invented locally. Each concentrated on their stand of trees and missed the wood.

The main problem was that, despite the assurances given in the earlier study terms of reference, it had not proved possible to limit the scope of the service management activities to just the IT Services division. When we came to examine and describe the individual service management processes and functions, the dependencies, particularly between 'operations' and 'development' but also between 'operations' and 'administration' became clear. Not that those dependencies were denied; in fact they had almost become peripheral to the argument because what had assumed an overwhelming importance was the question of organisational control.

'The question is,' said Humpty Dumpty, 'which is to be master – that's all.'

And the fiercest battles centred around the question of the relationship with the directorate's customers. This had traditionally been the province of the software developers and maintainers. Their past products were after all in a state of constant change, with some major services suffering a daily amendment cycle. Their relationship – sometimes with a precursor to the *intelligent customer* within the business areas served – was comfortable, or well-established, or simply important to their parochial needs and ambitions.

A set of fundamental beliefs

The problem with ITIL is that, while not a method to be slavishly followed in its application, it nevertheless has to be treated as an entity. It has a single structure, a single set of fundamental beliefs. And these are not to do with its organisational implementation but with the relationship that should (must) exist between service provider and service recipient. At its very heart, we came to believe, were the following precepts:

♥ that responsibility and authority for delivering a service must coexist

♥ that the only sensible view of a service was one that encompassed every stage and activity of its life, from conception to death.

'When I use a word,' Humpty Dumpty said in a rather scornful tone, 'it means just what I choose it to mean – neither more nor less.'

We also came to believe that the language of ITIL was an important factor in establishing a common understanding of how services should be managed but that this created its own difficulties, particularly among those who had not the inclination (or opportunity) to learn the language for themselves. So, the lesson we learned was that enthusiasm was vital for cohesion within the project and fine for the clients – they welcomed being spoken to as customers – but that it must be tempered when negotiating with other IT staff if unnecessary conflict is to be avoided.

7.4 So, what happened next?

It is now the beginning of 1992. The directorate's eight month freeze on recruitment, imposed during 1991 while some departmental organisational changes took place, is over. Why it was thought necessary to interrupt a planned reduction of staff numbers I'll never understand!

'… and your hair has become very white'.

Phase 2 of the project is underway. This involves pursuing a number of common activities for the establishment of each ITIL function such as Problem

Management, Change Management, etc. Recognising that this was a substantial IT organisation but nevertheless understanding that one 'functional manager' does not necessarily equal one person, the common tasks were:

♣ appoint a functional manager

(Quite a lot of thought was given to who might best fit a function or number of functions, based on the BCS Industry Structure Model, Release 2. However, some candidates who were considered 'ideal' didn't want to do that particular job – and there was not actually an infinite choice!)

♣ identify staff to be trained and arrange suitable training

(This was easier. All managerial staff (HEO and above) attended ISEB accredited Service Management training courses – mainly at the Civil Service College. Some PRINCE® training also took place.)

♣ produce a Mission Statement and a definition of the rôles, requirements and responsibilities of staff

(This turned out to be a much more substantial exercise than first envisaged and resulted in the production of a complete set of 'Functional Descriptions', covering every aspect of Service Management. These are described later.)

♣ review the current processes, procedures and 'desk instructions' and define detailed new management and clerical procedures as well as any changed accommodation and environmental requirements

(Much of this work had been completed during a generic gap analysis and reporting exercise.)

♣ mount an awareness campaign

*'I have answered three questions, and that is enough …
Do you think I can listen all day to such stuff?'*

(This was something that we didn't manage at all well. We were never quite sure what it was and in any case really didn't have – or thought we didn't have – the resources or skills to do it properly. This was a mistake! An awareness campaign, mounted for the benefit of internal IT staff as well as for the customers would have been a golden opportunity to isolate the dissenters and force a reconciliation of views and objectives before we had progressed too far. The later interruptions to progress because of silly battles over 'what is a configuration item and does a mouse have to be identified separately?' or major battles over where the Customer Account Manager sits might then have been avoided.)

♣ test tools and clerical procedures before bringing the function into service

♣ introduce effective, timely and accurate management reporting and plan for the function to evolve to meet changing business needs and for periodic reviews of its efficiency and effectiveness.

(It had already been decided that information not required for decision making had no permanent value.)

Other tasks

In addition to these individual activities, there were a number of general tasks. These were:

♦ carry out a procurement exercise to identify and procure the most suitable software support tools

♦ buy the appropriate hardware to run them on

♦ monitor and manage the overall implementation of ITIL processes.

During this phase, one of the biggest problems was that of balancing skilled and scarce staff resources. Inevitably, there turned out to be only a small number of key players, at various levels in the organisation – the sort of people that you rely on to keep things going as well as to develop the new schemes.

Now, here, you see, it takes all the running you can do to keep in the same place. If you want to get somewhere else, you must run at least twice as fast as that!

And the world did not stop turning, neither could the department escape being involved in national 'exercises'. So the balance between the old and the new shifted many times in favour of the old: that was, after all, where our current customer commitments resided and, frustrating as it was for progress, it was clear where our duty lay. The alternative approach of separating the old from the new entirely was never considered feasible. Too much was changing and we knew we had to take account of, and learn from, the new in order to create a strong and flexible management framework for the future.

That need for flexibility was also unsettling for those involved. While they accepted that a new furrow was being ploughed, their natural preference was for a reasonable measure of stability. It was not always possible to supply this, particularly in terms of the organisational structure within the IT Services division, given that we were learning all the time. And of course there were still the management battles being fought. However, there were periods of relative peace!

'Let's fight till six, and then have dinner,' said Tweedledum.

7.5 And then came market testing ...

I only took the regular course ... the different branches of Arithmetic – Ambition, Distraction, Uglification and Derision.

Market testing, mainly because it was followed fairly quickly by the directorate's move towards agency status, caused relatively little impact. In order to defuse potential internal arguments (which might have lead to further delay) we commissioned a short independent consultancy study to ensure that nothing that was being done or planned in the infrastructure management project would conflict with the move towards market testing. The report, delivered in February 1993, concluded that not only were there no conflicts between the two objectives but that all the work now being undertaken was a proper precursor to a successful market testing project. It did, however, point out that, with the skills available, the infrastructure project target dates were too ambitious and should be phased – partly to demonstrate the tangible improvements already accomplished; and that the close association between ITIL and ISO 9000 should be further explored.

The report also highlighted the progress made towards developing a service management strategy for the directorate as a whole.

The spring and summer of 1993 were spent furthering that aim and producing one of the most important set of documents to emerge from the project, which comprised

♠ the Functional Specifications

♠ the Catalogue of Customer Services

♠ the Standard Code of Practice (SCOP).

(This was the document designed to sit above the SLAs and contain all the non-service specific information customers would require.)

Functional specifications

Discipline by discipline, the functional specifications described how the best practice guidance in ITIL translated into terms meaningful to our organisation. They explained in straightforward language what the function was, who was involved and what its mission statement was.

They then went on to set out, again in plain language.

♥ The objectives

(For the first time the task of those responsible for the delivery and support of live services was openly described in great detail.)

♥ the functional boundaries and interfaces – not just IT but covering the whole of the organisation

(Of crucial importance, this emphasised that everyone in the directorate had a rôle to play. It said plainly that there were no internal boundaries that were of the slightest interest to customers but it was nevertheless vital that all understood and accepted their individual or collective responsibilities.)

♥ the processes and procedures

(The functional specifications did not descend to the 'desk instruction' level but set out all the main procedural components.)

♥ the parameters by which that function would be measured

(As well as introducing the concept of functional efficiency and effectiveness reviews, this section, for the first time, started to describe the metrics that would be collected and used to ensure that the service management processes remained on track.)

♥ the skills and training required to carry out the function successfully.

(The skills described were based upon the BCS Industry Structure Model – soon to be re-published in its third release. ISEB Infrastructure Management: Service Management training was mandatory for all middle managers and above – though not all chose to take the examinations. Had it been available at the time, the ISEB/EXIN Service Management Foundation Certificate would also have been a firm requirement for the remaining staff.)

Managing relationships

The SCOP, again, proved to be something of a battleground for it aimed to describe the external services provided by the three constituent parts of the directorate and the nature and extent of the relationships they had with their clients. Also, importantly, how those relationships were to be managed in the future. The directorate had not before faced these issues and, like most other organisations not under threat, it had comfortably continued in what it would have described as a mature relationship with its users. From the outside, however, others saw it as old fashioned and ill-equipped to face the future. The SCOP provided the opportunity to discuss these issues, to develop a common understanding of through-life service management and to adopt a common approach. It was not entirely successful in achieving that aim. Perhaps language alone cannot persuade.

"'Then you should say what you mean,' the March Hare went on. 'I do,' Alice hastily replied; 'at least – at least I mean what I say – that's the same thing you know.'"

"'Not the same thing a bit!' said the Hatter. 'Why, you might just as well say that 'I see what I eat' is the same thing as 'I eat what I see!'"

7.6 So, where did it all end?

The answer, of course, is that a project such as I have described never really ends, it simply turns into a cycle of continuous improvement. So, the best that can be done is to describe what the project has achieved so far, and what it has not.

Change Management and Software Control and Distribution	The aim was to create a centralised change management process. This needed to embrace all parts of the directorate to be fully effective. Most of the resistance came from the software project teams – and a few customer sites. It was argued to be a bureaucratic bottleneck rather than an essential source of information in the fight to reduce the number and severity of service failures – most of which arose from change. There are still islands of resistance but the availability of good management information, including type, frequency and cost of changes, is turning the tide. A working Change Advisory Board, however, has still not yet been set up.
	Software release management has taken a step in the right direction with fewer unscheduled releases. This function has been closely allied with software technical support.
Problem Management and the Customer Service Desk (CSD)	Now working well, with excellent statistics being produced. An interim call logging system was created locally at the beginning of the project and proved to be a most valuable source of information and training. Among other things, it showed that it was unrealistic to aim for 90% of calls to be closed by CSD staff, 60% being nearer the mark. The difference between incidents and problems, and the need to separate their management, is well understood. The interface with Customer Account Management – which was recognised to be intimately associated with the CSD – continues to cause some difficulty. There also continues to be a danger of *intelligent customer* style clients not sharing 'their' service quality information, collected via their own 'Help Desks'.
Configuration Management	The data collection exercise proved to be most difficult. Issues of 'ownership' arose and insufficient authority was vested, publicly, in those responsible for the creation of the CMDB. Some third party assistance was bought in and this helped. The phasing of data capture is important since there has to be a close link established and maintained between Configuration Management and Change Management. The depth of data recording was not finally settled until it was pointed out that a box of toner for a laser printer (which did not have a discrete serial number) was more valuable than a PC keyboard! The real overhead in Configuration Management is not, of course, in labelling the equipment but in managing future change.

Service Level Management and Customer Account Management (CAM)	From the start, the CAM rôle failed to achieve the profile, authority or recognition that it deserved and required, mainly because the directorate continued to concentrate on the organisational, rather than functional, issues – who will control the CAMs and who will sign the SLAs rather than what is their purpose. In part, it was also due to the organisational culture of the government department in question. Consequently, some of the directorate's customers still do not understand the difference between a Service Level Requirement and a Service Level Agreement and service management still fails to be involved early enough in the service lifecycle. Other customers, however, have come to recognise the valuable contribution that Customer Account Managers can make and are now insisting on their presence during discussions and negotiations with the software developers. So, all in all, a much healthier state of affairs than existed before and well-worn phrases like 'customer focus' are beginning to ring true.
Cost Management	The first invoices have now been produced but, on the way, there have been a number of difficulties in ensuring that all financial information is recorded in a compatible format and to a common structure. The lesson to be learned here is that financial management staff need to be more fully involved from the beginning of such a project – and take a much greater responsibility for driving this aspect of service management. But, although it now seems obvious that everyone is, perhaps they did not consider themselves then to be part of the directorate's service delivery mechanism, more just a necessary administrative control function! We did not, at that time, tend to judge our worth on the contribution we made to our business value chain.
Capacity Management	With the use of modern UNIX-based software, this function is now playing a full rôle in helping to predict the future – as well as keeping an eye on current performance.
Availability Management	Perhaps too much emphasis initially was given to the inventorial aspects of the function, which is really more the province of Configuration Management. They have still to get to grips with issues of vendor quality and the provision of useful management information on the reliability of components and services. However, this

function will no doubt mature as more SLAs come on-stream.

7.7   Conclusion

It was once said that, unlike a detective novel, where the trick is to try and guess who did it, with ITIL you are left wondering 'has anyone done it?'

Well, the answer is yes, and in spite of the emphasis in this case study on what went wrong and why, the reality is that the project I have described can rightly claim to have been a success. It was a leading edge initiative with little in the way of previous practical experience to lean on. The statistics needed to prove its case to the doubters within the family could only come from implementing the ITIL functions and it was in this particular respect that the ISEB training proved to be such a boon.

Our decision not to implement service management tools before writing and gaining general acceptance of the functional specifications was fundamental to that success. Apart from anything else, it allowed the vicious circle of change/incident/problem to become widely understood. That is not to play down the invaluable contribution made by Ultracomp's Red Box software (our eventual choice) but to understand that the flexibility and power of such an integrated tool-set is both its greatest asset and its greatest weakness, if not managed with care.

As may be discerned from the preceding paragraphs, the majority of the problems encountered were those concerning internal IT relationships and, in the heat of battle, it was a pity that we in the project team underestimated the power of the customer to influence our collective service management attitudes. Perhaps, next time, a customer survey should appear earlier in the activity list!

There remains one more major goal to be achieved – ISO 9000 certification. But such solid foundations have been laid that when that final project objective is reached, all will know for sure that it is worth more than the paper it is written on. And of course the move to agency status has had a significant and beneficial impact upon the culture of the entire organisation. The competitive world into which the directorate has now moved demanded change in exchange for opportunity and the challenge has been taken up.

> *Just then flew down a monstrous crow,*
> *As black as a tar-barrel;*
> *Which frightened both the heroes so,*
> *They quite forgot their quarrel.*

Service management implementation

8   Service management implementation

This case study was provided by Ultracomp Ltd

8 Service management implementation

8.1 Introduction

Four years ago, the departments at Stockton Borough Council had low expectations of their IT department. Since the arrival of Graham Coe as IT manager, he has worked with and expanded his team to create a service culture and raise the profile of IT among the council as a whole. This case study illustrates how Graham and his IT team managed to achieve a complete transformation, and in the process, strengthen the in-house IT department's position against any competitive bids to do the job from outside suppliers and the part ITIL guidelines played in achieving this.

8.2 The way we were

Up to 1988, Stockton Borough Council received computing services from Cleveland County Council, a large user of IBM equipment. In 1988, the borough broke away from this arrangement and installed an ICL mainframe system, chosen because it ran a good portfolio of local government applications.

But by the time Graham Coe arrived as IT manager in November 1991, there was general level of dissatisfaction with IT. His customers were in some instances having to wait several minutes for responses on the system, requests for change were handled haphazardly, and among the council in general 'there was total disillusionment with IT'.

The IT department had fourteen staff, including five computer operators. 'The department was under-resourced and the machine (an ICL 3955) was overloaded,' says Graham Coe. 'There was no-long term planning and the staff were constantly firefighting. They never had time to do anything properly.'

8.3 Improving service to customers

Fast action was required, and Graham immediately advertised for eight new staff, in order, as he says, 'to buy time, achieve some level of stability, and to address the customers' problems'. There were 300 applicants for the eight jobs, and so he managed to take on the best and most appropriate to his needs. All of them have stayed with the council.

The net result of these actions was to create some good will among the rest of the council. 'The customers could start to see an immediate improvement. They started to understand what we were trying to do. They were not as aggressive, even though the service was not measurably better yet. They could see little bits being added and improved.'

Having won approval from the council for a new way of running IT, he upgraded the system to an ICL 3965 in June 1992, and in late 1992, set about making improvements to the way the department ran its affairs. Graham had experience of installing costing and charging systems, unattended operations and disaster recovery, and he made these his first goals at Stockton. 'It was not a co-ordinated plan at the time. It was just common sense and gut feeling,' he admits, 'I knew I could make an impact on this council without costing them money. I could create a department that was lean and mean, while delivering the service, and all for £30,000 less a year.'

What turned this personal crusade into a more co-ordinated approach was a chance visit to a meeting of the Ultracomp Scottish Users Group, where Graham heard someone talking about ITIL and accreditation to the Information Systems Examinations Board (ISEB). 'I'd never heard of it,' Graham admits, but among the titles of the books referred to by the speaker, he recognised many of the ideas he had arrived at independently. 'I'd found something I had been looking for but thought was not there, a standard of work that could be accredited to show what you can do.'

On returning to Stockton, he immediately sent two staff on Ultracomp's Service Management course to achieve the ISEB Certificate of Proficiency in IT Infrastructure Management. Both were successful, and this also helped to raise awareness of the benefits that could be gained from introducing the appropriate working practices defined in the ITIL guidelines.

8.4   The threat of CCT

In early 1993, the in-house IT department had some 'serious worries' about the threat of Compulsory Competitive Tendering (CCT). Stockton IT department is the newest of the north-eastern authorities and as such felt it could be a target for outside bids. They were determined to pre-empt the threat, by taking a dispassionate look at the service they were providing, finding the weaknesses and fixing them. 'As a team, we took a strong look at ourselves and came up with a framework and a series of business plans. It wasn't funny and it wasn't pleasant. But we identified all the weaknesses,' recalls Graham Coe.

The exercise also produced a report setting out how information is handled and how business unit planning is done, and this has now become the standard reference work for the council's newly created Information Systems Steering Group. One of the areas that needed urgent action was the *Help Desk*, and the council looked at a number of packages before settling on Red Box from Ultracomp. Those staff who had been on the ISEB training courses were well qualified to identify the facilities and functionality required of an integrated service management solution, and to test how well the package performed and how closely it conformed to the ITIL guidelines. 'The need for an integrated service management toolkit was an afterthought,' says Graham Coe, 'We had only looked at Help Desk in isolation up to this point. Now we knew we needed to integrate other disciplines such as configuration management and change management, which not many packages handled to ITIL conformance.'

The Help Desk went live in May 1994, followed by Configuration Management – 'which is still not complete and never will be'– and then Change Management, which is now being implemented and expanded to cover more areas of activity.

On disaster recovery, a great deal of progress has been made, especially considering the council had no recovery plans when Graham Coe arrived. They have completed three successful tests now, but he still sees ways of making the plan even more watertight. Therefore, by May 96, he intends that disaster recovery tests will be carried out entirely by an outside organisation. He makes the point that it is foolish to rely totally on anyone from inside the council to handle any part of the plan: 'You need to able to plan for the unfortunate situation of your own staff not being available following a disaster.' The whole thing will be handled and tested externally, as it should be – 'and that isn't in the (ITIL) book', he observes.

This last piece of the disaster recovery plan could have been done this year, but the last test, monitored by an Ultracomp consultant, showed twenty-four points that needed fixing. One of these was an apparently simple point, that part of the recovery relied on having a VME operating system expert to hand. The IT team plan to rewrite this part of the manual so that anyone can follow it. Next time, they will make sure staff with no VME experience can handle that part of the recovery process.

ITIL has become the guiding light for the development of service management and the full set of books are to hand for regular reference. 'I believe that service management as advocated by ITIL is the key to winning CCT. And I want to make sure I don't lose,' says Graham Coe. For this reason, last October he underwent an outside assessment to test how his department was conforming to the ITIL guidelines. They were assessed by Ultracomp, whose *Squares* service is an objective measure of performance using a combination of ITIL guidelines and practical experience as a benchmark.

Areas for improvement
The report identified a quantum leap in quality of service being delivered to the customer, but it also identified some areas for improvement. The assessment scored the relevance and performance of each activity out of 100, and some of the worst were as follows:

- 7 for Change Management

- 17 for Problem Management

- 25 for Capacity Management

- 20 for Service Level Management.

For example, under change management, the assessment found staff changing live code, not recording changes, and leaving no reversion path in case changes did not work. There was also no consistent approach among the three development teams and technical support team, each of whom would handle requests differently. In overall terms, the assessment made seventy-five recommendations for how to improve the service, each given a 1, 2 or 3 priority.

For each recommendation, the IT team then had to decide:

- do we accept it?

- who owns it?

- is it IT's responsibility?

For instance, business recovery is a corporate issue, and so has been moved under the control of the Information Systems Steering Group. Other issues, such as the keeping of terminal downtime statistics, which was raised in the *Squares* report, have been passed to the newly formed Customer Care Group, made up of IT people and customers. 'Because not all customers require the same level of information, I can't dictate they shall have terminal downtime statistics. If they want it, we'll provide it,' says Graham Coe.

The remaining recommendations were broken down into two categories:

- an action item – that can be done in a day or two, and does not need a plan

- a planning item – with a set number of activities over a given period of time, under change management control.

The master plan to attack those issues has now been produced, and the IT team will be concentrating their efforts on the worst score areas. In those areas where they achieved high scores, such as unattended operations with 72%, they realise that directing resources to get closer to 100% would be less effective.

8.5   The future

The immediate future will be taken up in implementing *Squares* recommendations and going through another 'mini-Squares' assessment to see how far they have progressed against agreed service improvement targets. One measure of success is seen in the PC support area, where the team has just been increased from one to two people to support a population of 230 PCs.

ITIL highlights that IT departments can become victims of their own success, and this is something the team at Stockton have experienced at first hand. Before the second person arrived (paid for by the user departments), the number of outstanding calls stood at around seventy. 'Logic says that those calls will go down,' says Graham Coe. But the opposite has happened. The Help Desk is used more, the number of outstanding calls now averages 100-plus, and he is feeling the need to increase the Help Desk staff further.

The success of the Help Desk operation has opened up new opportunities in the rest of the council and Red Box is going to be used more widely as a general complaints handling/service request system. Now, when someone calls to complain about the dustbins or the schools, the complaint will be logged in the Red Box system and escalated until it is resolved and answered. As Graham Coe says: 'Local government these days is about customer service.' The use of ITIL– and a good measure of common sense – has helped Stockton turn what seemed to be a helpless situation to one where IT is respected and valued as force for good in the council.

8.6 One final point – perception

Graham Coe knows that once he has fully implemented the ITIL principles as recommended in the *Squares* assessment, customer care will inevitably improve. But as he says, there is just one more ingredient to success, and that is how the service is perceived. The involvement of other parts of the council in the Information Systems Steering Group and Customer Care Group plays a part in getting the message across, but he has supplemented this with regular IT awareness days to raise the department's profile and regular presentations on public platforms.

This marketing is having an effect. He is constantly playing host to other councils who want to see how Stockton are managing their affairs. This enhances the reputation of the council as a whole and hopefully will cause FM companies to look elsewhere for their business. As Graham Coe says: 'Stockton has had enough kicks in the past – now it is time for some credit marks. And the councillors like kudos, they like pats on the back, as do the staff involved in delivering the service. When they hear that other councils, much larger than us, now visit to see how we do things, then that increases the feel good factor.'

'From an IT viewpoint, ITIL has helped generate a lean, mean service environment focused on delivering a competitive service. Obviously the advent of CCT has been a motivating factor, but it goes beyond just winning the contract. It is about having everyone, regardless of job position, working together and being obsessed with providing a service second to none.' The greatest benefit of following the ITIL guidelines for service management is that the IT department's 'users' – viewed previously with distrust and irritation – have now become 'customers' working in conjunction with the IT team to deliver an efficient and consistent level of service to the community.

Disaster recovery planning

9 Disaster recovery planning

*This case study was provided by
Ultracomp Ltd*

9   Disaster recovery planning

9.1   Introduction

If it has ever been true that local government was a sleepy backwater, that is certainly not the case now. Local authorities work to tight budgets, and individual departments must be prepared to brave the rigours of compulsory competitive tendering. They are fighting for their lives. Central to achieving many of these goals is the need to have efficient information systems for the management of local government finances. But greater reliance on computers begs the obvious question: what do you do when they go wrong? Four years ago St Albans District Council set about tackling the problem, and began laying the foundations of a contingency plan which could ensure that, whatever happened, the Council would be able to continue to do its work effectively and serve the community.

**9.2   The need for a
Contingency Plan**

Four years ago, St Albans District Council had only recently installed its own ICL mainframe systems, having previously been served by a consortium with neighbouring Watford Borough Council.

The Council placed a high priority on disaster recovery, especially given the growing pressure on local government to perform like a business and the need to collect the new Community Charge (the so-called 'Poll Tax'). In addition, the need for a contingency plan was highlighted further by two terrorist incidents in St Albans close to the Council's offices. Martin Ferguson, IT Manager at St Albans, recalls that the Council carried out a simple business impact analysis across all departments of the Council to assess how each department would be affected by a loss of systems. 'You can go to all sorts of lengths with this impact analysis. Essentially, ours was very simple, looking at each of the main applications on the mainframe and then discussing with the users the practical requirements of each of these applications, prioritising them and determining what sort of back-up they needed in terms of hot and cold start, or simply manual alternatives.'

Since all the main financial systems resided on the mainframe system, it made sense to provide immediate back-up by making arrangements with both hot-start and cold-start suppliers of mainframe services. Hot-start suppliers specialise in making a system immediately available to carry out urgent jobs while the customer's own system is temporarily out of service; cold start suppliers cater for the more serious long-term breakdown (such as the loss of a building), where a replacement machine may have to be supplied for a period of time, possibly in a temporary computer room. St Albans initially evaluated the Hot Start options and found three possible suppliers.

Price was naturally a factor in choosing the services, but Martin Ferguson was eager to choose a company that would work well with his own staff, particularly in the stressful situation of a disaster. 'We wanted the staff to feel comfortable with the whole environment and the procedures they had to follow to recover systems. We involved a lot of our staff in selecting our supplier.' They made a short list of two, and asked them to do a dry-run exercise to see how they coped with taking Council files and running them on their own machines.

The tests were quite conclusive and as a result ACT was chosen as the hot-start supplier. In addition, Comdisco was chosen as the cold-start supplier for the provision of longer-term cover.

9.3   Business continuity

But as Martin Ferguson concedes, replacing the mainframe is 'a fairly minimalist view of disaster recovery planning'. You have to move on into contingency planning, looking at the wider issues of an organisation and the services it provides. The approach up to that point had been pragmatic and geared to putting in the basic back-up the Council would need if the mainframe stopped. 'Politically, we felt this was a priority,' says Martin Ferguson. So once the hot- and cold-start facilities had been put in place, St Albans started working closely with the software and consultancy company Ultracomp to put together a more complete business continuity plan. Ultracomp consultant Vernon Lloyd, who worked with them during that period, takes up the story: 'We began by using the proforma plan straight from the ITIL book, and filled in the blanks for the specific site.'

'The ITIL guide to disaster recovery', he says, 'acted as an excellent reference list of everything that needed to be covered, from listing the telephone numbers of everyone who would need to contacted in an emergency, and who would be responsible for what, to the relevant insurance requirements.'

'As the plan evolved, it became more of a working document,' says Vernon Lloyd. The document developed to fit the specific requirements of St Albans, and grew away from the original proforma document. 'It made a very good starting point for writing a plan, but it is only meant as a guideline,' he says.

The current plan defines everything that needs to be done for each level of emergency, escalating response according to the seriousness of the problem. Martin Ferguson is the owner of the plan and is ultimately responsible for its effectiveness. But as part of their on-site duties Ultracomp manage the plan, and ensure that if any changes occur (even someone's home telephone number), the master plan is updated and new sheets are sent out to each holder of a copy so that their copies are right up to date.

Coverage

The main areas covered by the plan are:

- the business requirements for disaster recovery

- the essential services covered by the plan, with their recovery priority ratings

- the contingency planning team members, and their duties

- a list of all the names (of both individuals and organisations) with their telephone numbers and addresses

- a description for disaster detection and impact assessment up to the point of invoking the plan

- a detailed description of the disaster recovery procedures, including return to the original location after the emergency is over

- guidelines on salvaging equipment from the disaster site and arranging cleaning and repair, with details of possible contractors

- all insurance policy details

- procedures to adopt following failure of air conditioning or power supplies

- procedures to follow whenever changes occur that could affect the contingency plan.

9.4   **Testing the plan**

An essential prerequisite of any plan is that it should be tested regularly. St Albans tests its own plan annually, with Ultracomp acting as an independent assessor to document any shortcomings in the plan, or to record where the plan is not followed. If the mainframe system is brought to a halt, the back-up files kept in fireproof safes at a central depot two miles away are transported to the ACT site in Portsmouth. Provided the Council buildings are useable, the staff can access the ACT machine from their terminals and PCs, as they would normally. In the event of a major disaster affecting the offices, then the staff would move to a central depot where there is ample office space. There is also some provision for staff to take over desk space in Portsmouth, although this would be kept to a minimum.

In the tests, the IT team has tried to be as realistic as possible, but has not gone as far as shutting down the main systems completely while the contingency procedure kicks into action. 'The annual test is currently focused on the mainframe. We learnt a lot from our early annual tests and always have a debriefing session to identify what needs to be done to improve the plan,' says Ferguson.

The tests have always worked, although they have always thrown up problems to be ironed out, as Ferguson recalls: 'One early problem that we identified was that our low speed link to Portsmouth was not good enough and we have since installed an ISDN2 link at the central depot to speed up communication between Portsmouth and St Albans.' Some work has also been done to ensure that the Finance Department's plans dovetail with those of the IT department. 'We tightened up a lot of the tape handling routines for our Unix systems and also the whole area of PC back-up was improved at both ends,' says Ferguson.

With the Unix systems the departmental link officers load the tapes and take them to the off-site depot. PCs are the responsibility of the user to ensure they have adequate back-up, and they have the service of a tape streamer back-up device. 'Depending on how critical their systems are they will back-up more or less frequently. At the moment we allow them to decide but that could change further down the track if we get into networked PCs. '

9.5 Future plans

Martin Ferguson strongly favours the notion of the *intelligent customer* – the capability within the business for working with the IT department to set the direction for the use of IS and IT rather than the passive reception of services. He says: 'It changes the role of the IT function from purely providing a kind of technical solution to being a facilitator and enabler, working with and educating the customer. As time goes on the complexity of the requirement increases as you start to build in a lot of other issues such as the culture of the organisation, internal procedures of departments, and the way the services are delivered. That way we can start to expand out from focusing purely on the mainframe to office systems generally, whether they happen to be on mainframe or distributed systems – or manual systems for that matter. And that's when life starts to get quite interesting.'

This wider thinking makes the whole organisation more aware of contingency planning, and in St Albans case, has prompted the extension of information systems into new arenas.

Martin Ferguson again: 'You realise the importance of document image systems and geographic information systems (GIS). At the moment, all our maps are kept in hard copy on the first floor and that's it, no back-up whatsoever. It's the same with microfiche where we have just one copy in the offices somewhere. The same goes for historical records. There is no back-up. With document image systems and GIS we can have off-site back-up with files locked away in fireproof safes.'

The process that started off as mainframe back-up, has therefore spread its boundaries to all areas of the Council. 'We have raised the level of awareness and understanding about the need for contingency planning within the authority as a whole and we have a commitment to it now across the authority,' says Ferguson. But he is also realistic: 'Getting commitment turned into action is another matter. The approach we are adopting is to bite off a bit at a time. We started in the Finance Department – they have their own contingency plan now for their accounting and financial services and they now have one for their revenue's side of the business. We are in the process of looking for the next bit to bite off. We shall gradually build up a jigsaw of plans to cover the whole authority. The other issue that arises then is to pull them all together corporately.'

9.6   The verdict on ITIL   All parties agree the ITIL guidelines made an excellent point of departure for mapping out a business continuity plan. But Martin Ferguson's view is: 'The framework provided by the ITIL guidelines served the purpose of directing our thinking into all the various technical and non-technical areas of contingency planning. We then overlaid this on our own site-specific requirements to ensure the completeness of the plan.'

ITIL support for IT service quality improvement

10 ITIL support for IT service quality improvement

This case study was provided by
The Quint Wellington Redwood Group

10 ITIL support for IT service quality improvement

*Rules are for the guidance of wise men
and the obedience of fools.*

The truth is rarely pure, and never simple.
Oscar Wilde

10.1 Just books and bureaucracy

ITIL, IPW™ and ISO 9000 are recognised means of improving an IT Services organisation. But do they just represent a lot of books, a lot of bureaucratic rules and procedures, a lot of work – work that is of no immediate value to the customer? Can they really lead to higher service quality?

We think they can, but only indirectly. ITIL, IPW and ISO 9000 are the means of creating a structure for working practices; a structure that is consistent and effective, one that ensures strong organisational direction and reduces the possibility of getting side-tracked.

But the structure itself is not a service quality improvement, it is only a framework for quality improvement. Nevertheless, the expectations of ITIL in this respect continue to be high. Sometimes too high.

This case study is the story of what we believe to be the largest ITIL implementation in the world, why we did it and what we have learned.

10.2 The company

The subject of this case study is a major telecommunications company. It has one of the largest IT departments in the country and their main goal is to provide information services to all of the different business units within the company as well as dealing with the underlying technical aspects of business automation. The company is divided into business oriented units. These are in turn divided into a number of widely spread 'working units' and some central staff units responsible for deciding how the business should be run and what products are to be sold.

The IT department supports all these functions and is itself divided into five branches, each responsible for managing a different IT platform. There are four main computing centres, one for IBM mainframes, one for Digital, one for Unisys and HP and one for Tandem architectures. There is also a centre, called the End User

113

Service Department, that services the LANs/WANs and the Office Automation customers. Each of these centres supports a different aspect of the company's core business. In 1992, more than 2000 people were working in IT departments and the total number of customers was in excess of 30,000. When the company decided to use ITIL as the basis for its organisational improvements it was, without doubt, the biggest project of its kind in the world.

10.3 ... but why change the basic way of working?

As competition gets tougher, the demands placed on the IT department get stronger. In this case, the direct message from the company was: provide a better quality of service and handle more work with the same or a fewer number of people or ...

This caused some of the IT managers to start searching for solutions to the problems they now faced. The demand was for more throughput, better predictions, higher overall quality, wider responsibilities, greater flexibility – but everything against a need to reduce costs.

The manager of the Digital site searched for methods to deal with the data centre problem. He came across lots of models and methods for software development, project management etc, but nothing dealing with the entire service lifecycle. It might have been easy at that stage to argue that his service centre was unique, that there was a good case for going his own way, that the different technology and culture of his department justified this. Then he came across ITIL. His first reaction was, I could have thought of this myself, but I haven't had to, so it is good.

The fundamental questions that ITIL was going to have to solve were:

- Could we build a structure in our service centres that allowed room for flexibility?

- Could we improve the quality of our work, not by involving more people in extra checks but by embedding quality into the natural workflow?

- Could we operate, survive and be successful in a competition-oriented world, against market-oriented prices?

- Were we capable of managing this new type of organisation, now and in the future?

10.4 Did ITIL seem like a good bet?

In the first place ITIL was chosen because there was no real alternative. ITIL was attractive because it was pragmatic and because it contained a lot of supporting detail for the practical implementation of the various Service Management functions.

But there were also a lot of volumes! Clearly it was unrealistic to expect everyone to read the books, hope that they would do what was in them and then expect a successful outcome. What was missing was an overall view of the processes that needed to be managed. Yet it was obvious that was going to be necessary to implement ITIL in a highly controlled and structured manner – in the same way in which any major organisational change should be managed.

10.5 So, before we started ...

The lesson learned from earlier ITIL experiences and from other companies was that it is impossible to implement ITIL as though one were implementing Encyclopædia Britannica. What was required was a model, against which we could examine the most important functions in IT, those which were expensive in people and specialist skills. But we did not want to make the same mistake that a lot of IT companies had made by starting with talking about ITIL and the organisational structure to support it. We knew that would end up in endless discussions about functions and responsibilities, about who rather than what. We therefore decided to take the approach of defining the most important IT processes that supported the overall quality of the services. But even before we talked about the processes, we thought about how and in what steps the project should be managed. We chose the following implementation strategy model.

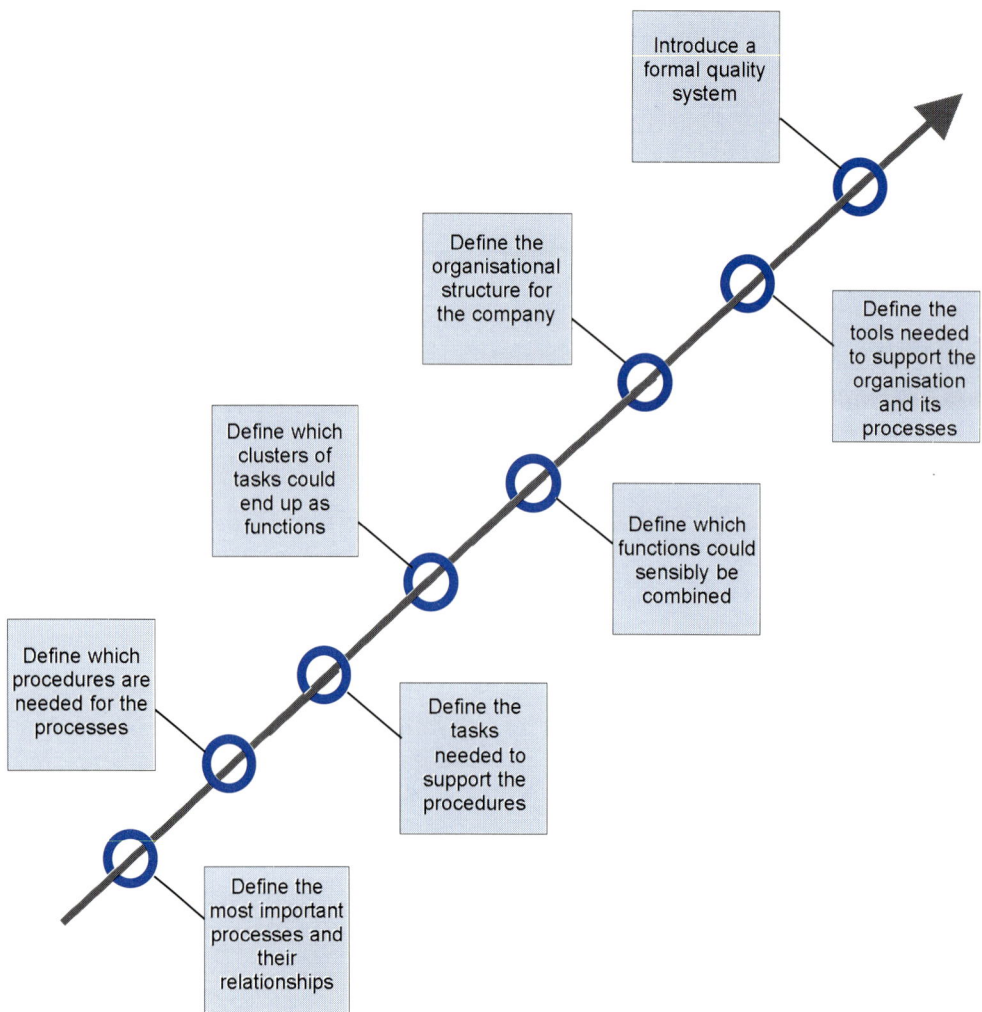

Figure 10.1: Implementation strategy model

This simple structure defines the steps that we followed in order to ensure the successful completion of our IT organisational improvement project. It was preceded by an analysis phase where, by questionnaire and other techniques, we established the existing Service Management baseline. The first three steps then became known as the 'unfreeze' phase, the next four the 'reconfigure' phase and the final step the 'refreeze' phase.

We already knew that implementing Service Management was not simply the implementation of a number of sets of procedures but the implementation of a complex set of interdependent processes. Because of this it was very important to recognise that the implementation of Service Management would require changes in working methods, changes in culture and, eventually, changes in organisational structure. Each of these would require a good deal of attention but the order in which we dealt with them was crucial. But how to define a generic process model that could be used to improve the quality of all of the services?

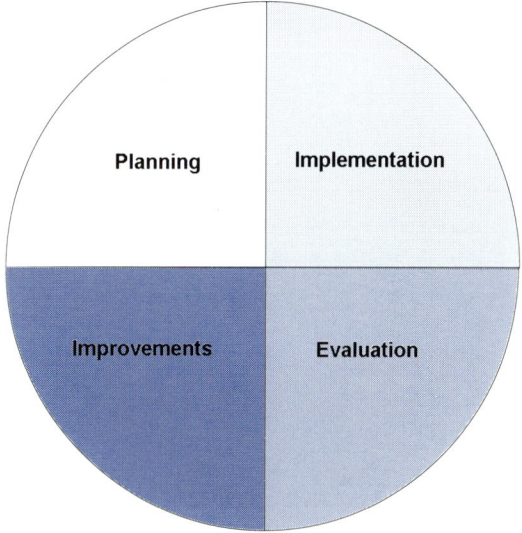

Figure 10.2: The quality circle

Quality improvement: the IPW model

Since quality models are very well known in manufacturing we went to see how they did it. It seemed that the most important concern in a factory was the continuity of quality improvement. In order to guarantee quality it needed to be designed into the day-to-day production cycle. For this they used the quality circle, then designed working processes which supported that quality circle. After careful examination, we concluded that we could not define our processes directly with the use of ITIL. We recognised that ITIL would provide a great deal of help at the procedure and work instruction levels but it said little about the processes in combination with a quality model. So before we progressed further and in order to secure a generic working model, we had to define the ITIL processes within a quality circle. What emerged from that work was the beginning of the process model which became known as IPW (Implementation of Process-oriented Workflow).

10.6   IPW

IPW is the standardised implementation of the ITIL processes. It deals with every aspect of IT Service Management, the processes, procedures, tasks, functional responsibilities, documentation, organisational concerns and support tools.

In its full form, it encompasses the complete range of Service Support and Delivery functions as well as software development, customer account management and the production environment – and contains all of the required data links. However, the simplified IPW process model with which we started to map out the processes of Production, Incident Management, Problem Management and Change looked like this:

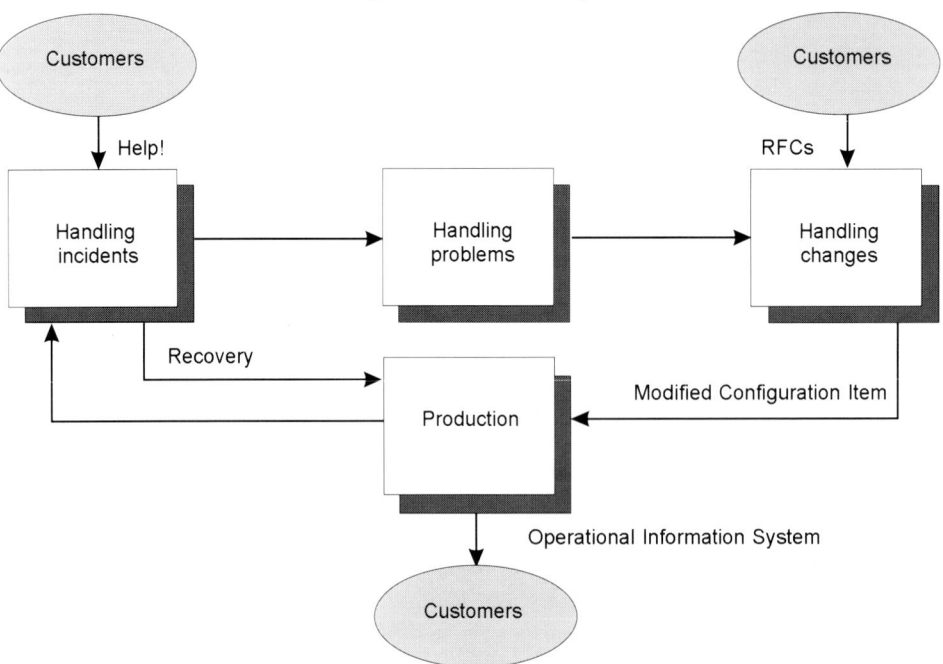

Figure 10.3: IPW process model

The strength of IPW is that it translates ITIL from the books to the real life working situation. You cannot read IPW, you can only do it.

The major problem in many IT organisations is lack of clarity. Everyone seems to be involved in everything. Yet when things go wrong, it is always so difficult to pin down the responsibility for putting them right again. The majority of IT staff are dealing with incidents and changes and many will have direct contact with the customers. Staff are usually technically well-grounded and motivated but none are able to attach an accurate relative priority, either to their firefighting duties or to their routine work. And seldom do they learn from others during the careful process of passing the refuse bin on to next door.

What was so important about ITIL and the IPW model in this project was that they made individuals aware of their rôle in the different processes, free from concerns about company organisational structure. Also, where one process stopped, its output became the input for the next process so it was clear what the input and output boundaries and expectations were. IPW clarified the contact points and moments between the IT staff and the customers; working and thinking in processes broke down the walls between departments – walls which had existed for as long as anyone could remember.

10.7   Production

Production is the process that gets carried out when nothing happens to disturb it! Of course it *is* the single process that provides benefit to the customer; provides what has been asked for; maybe even provides what is described in a Service Level Agreement. If the systems are available, the customer can log in, enter data, manipulate stored information, reach conclusions, make informed decisions, produce a printout, etc. However ...

... the production process is constantly threatened with things going wrong. And it is at that point that incident management starts.

Incident management deals with every kind of service interruption. Interruptions varying from a simple, forgotten password, up to the total loss of an information system network. Our first goal was to minimise the impact of the incident on customers by restoring the service as soon as possible, or at least giving them a good workaround. Incident solving was something that we were good at. After all, we were always doing it. We did it over and over again, hardly seeming to learn from our mistakes.

We therefore needed a form of problem solving that removed, once and for all, the root causes of repetitive incidents. Problem Management does this. Looking through the incident database we started to find incidents with similar symptoms, or configuration items that seemed to give rise to more than their fair share of incidents or customer groups who appeared to be suffering more than an average number of failures. It did not take long to find the weak spots in our IT infrastructure environment. Problem Management then helped to define the solutions.

A second aspect that constantly threatens the production process is change. We were trying to improve the quality of the infrastructure all the time, suppliers launched their new versions of hardware and software – often it seemed before full use had been made of the old ones – and customers needed new applications, improved functionality and everything faster than before. Formal Change Management gave us a tremendous opportunity to keep that constant flow of changes controlled; to implement them in the right order, after proper analysis and planning, with clear communication between all the parties involved and, finally, at the lowest possible risk of production failure.

10.8 A place for everything …

However, we knew that none of this would run automatically. Everyone had to have their place in each of these processes. We therefore described the processes in outline so that there was no uncertainty as to where the process boundaries lay. We then divided them into smaller and smaller steps. First we devised the accompanying procedures, describing which departments were involved at what point in the procedure, who was responsible, who was actually carrying out that procedure and who had to be kept informed. Then how the output of one set of tasks was to provide the input for the next one. At the end of this stage, we had described the 200 or so activities that needed to be carried out in the service centre.

Then we re-grouped those activities into logical units (tasks). Management activities, such as progress control, quality control and reporting we grouped into various managers' functions. And, to ensure that the boundaries remained clear within the organisation, we called them Incident Manager, Problem Manager and Change Manager, each of them ultimately responsible for the management of that process though not necessarily managing all of the resources being utilised.

The activities that dealt with capacity planning and the engaging and controlling of people were grouped into department managers' functions. And so we created each of the functions in turn, ensuring that every defined process, procedure and task was placed in one or more functions, and if in more than one, that the boundaries of responsibility were kept crystal clear.

Configuration Management

After we had developed the IPW process model it was easy to build procedures and work instructions with the help of the ITIL books. What we had learned from our discussions about the model was that Configuration Management is not the first function you should be concerned about. From just reading the ITIL modules it seems that you can not do anything without Configuration Management. However, we decided to tackle Configuration Management last, after we had substantially completed our work on the main Service Support processes. In that way, we would not have to face the risk of drowning in Configuration Management data before producing something really useful to the IT Services organisation. We could not avoid some of the Configuration Management connotations of the IPW processes but we did not suffer from the common mistake of appearing to be filling in Configuration Management data for its own sake and then struggling to maintain its validity.

10.9   The first implementation

After a lot of discussions about the IPW model we had decided that its great value lay in allowing us to clarify the true rôle of the IT Infrastructure Library, that is at the procedure and work instruction level. We then started to build a company quality model that looked like that shown overleaf.

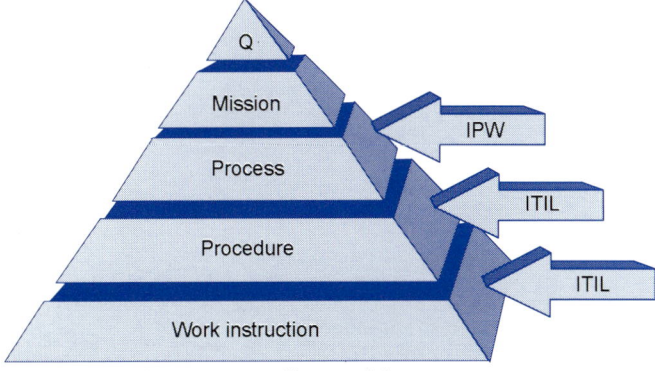

Figure 10.4: Company quality model

10.10   Lessons about restructuring

To implement this corporate quality model we had to restructure the way many of our IT employees worked. To achieve this we thought that we had only to arrange a few workshops. After a couple of weeks it became apparent that more regular workshops were needed and, when the final score was counted we found that we had carried out more than sixty. Looking back, it is clear that it was these workshops that did the trick. We have learned that implementing these models is only possible if you are able to change the culture of working. Managing the project in a way that recognised and supported that culture change saved the implementation. Within eleven months we had a restructured Digital Data Centre which employed service oriented work methods instead the old functional and hierarchic approach.

10.11 Checking the results

Because the company wanted to check how well this new way of working was implemented and measure the results, the management of the IT department arranged for an external audit of the project to be carried out. To do this, they brought in the quality experts from Det Norske Veritas. The results were astounding. By using ITIL as a means of achieving high quality and stable procedures and desk instructions within an IPW process model that itself contributed to a quality circle, the overall score recorded by Det Norske Veritas was 72% on the ISO 9002 scale. It seemed that without knowing much about ISO 9000 we had invented a quality system for IT, based on ITIL.

10.12 The morning after

When published, the audit report created a huge motivational peak within the company, and because of the degree of ISO compliance resulting from use of the IPW model, the company's management decided to introduce identical projects into all the other data centres. After a year, every data centre was well on the way to implementing Service Management based on ITIL. The projects were relatively problem-free until …

… it became noticeable that there were problems with the integration of the services from different data centres. Individually, Change and Problem Management were working well but there was no co-ordination or flow of information between sites. However, as time went on more and more desk-level applications were using the background applications and these were run at different data centres, each of which had their own particular direct clients as well as this more general responsibility. Carrying out Change Management, for example, on the general use hardware and software posed a number of new problems. One of these was that the background applications had their own direct users with their own service level expectations. So who owned the application, who paid for the application and who was to be given priority? To overcome these problems it was decided that there should be a new range of Service Level Agreements and a new way of working between the data centres.

Another problem arose from the introduction of ISO 9002 in that it created a tendency towards bureaucracy. More and more people were saying 'today I have to concentrate on ISO 9002, tomorrow I go back to work'. People saw the introduction of ISO 9002, combined with IPW and ITIL, as work in its own right, losing sight of their real day-to-day jobs. This way of thinking became even more pervasive after the introduction of the Quality and Procedure Handbooks. The mistake that was made was letting the central staff specialists write these books instead of asking the people whose day-to-day job it was. The tendency of the 'specialists' is to record everything on paper and we therefore ended up with books of more than 200 pages. It was being said that you could even hire a monkey to do the work, providing he or she could read!

Happily this was recognised in the project before too many resources had been wasted and that particular approach was stopped. The Quality and Procedure Handbooks then became much slimmer and staff recognised that they were working within a quality system, not on one.

10.13 The final hurdle

By this time, only one of the IT departments had not yet made the leap and the final goal of the project was to implement Service Management, with IPW as its process model, for the End User Service Department.

This department was huge; some 15,000 terminals or PCs and about 120 LANs spread across 17 different locations. Its size and complexity always represented the major hurdle we would, eventually, have to overcome. Introducing formal Service Management into a decentralised department has to be done very carefully, particularly so if there is no single centre of executive control. Added to which, there was the problem that most of the end user IT services originated from one or other of the technical data centres and were being delivered through a complex web of client/server facilities. Clearly the implementation of full Service Management within this department was only going to be possible with top corporate management commitment. We knew enough at that stage to realise that attempting to deliver a service of that planned quality without controlling processes underlying the service was a waste of time.

The franchise approach

However, no further organisational changes were to be permitted, so for the first time, we had to deal with Service Management staff who were not 'ours'. We looked around to see how other organisations tackled this problem and concentrated our research on two, McDonalds and the Post Office. What was particularly interesting about each of these was that they had based their internal control mechanisms upon the franchise concept. With a franchise, the central control mechanisms have to ensure corporate quality while not owning the local means of delivery. This is managed, not through a mass of detailed contracts, but through the agreement and issuing of service formulae, formulae that might govern how a customer is to be greeted, how to deal with complaints, how to sell a telephone, what onions or other 'service components' to buy, etc. In this way, the centre is able to influence, effectively control, the manner in which the service is delivered without having to be 'in charge' of the people concerned.

We were not a franchised organisation of course but we set up a formula section and, with the end user departments, constructed a set of organisational rules and procedures that would serve exactly the same purpose. This section effectively designed the way the service was to be delivered in each of the seventeen other departments.

In order for those seventeen sites to carry out their local Service Management responsibilities to a common standard, a great deal of time had to be spent on communication and training. Each of the local Problem (which included incident) Management and Change Management cells were integrated into the corporate Problem and Change Management process and over-arching Problem and Change Advisory Boards were set up. Each of these was chaired by the Change/Problem Manager in the central End User Service Department and all of the seventeen 'free-standing' Change/Problem

124

Management functions were represented. Naturally, only problems or changes with corporate wide implications were discussed. We were certainly not in the business of bureaucracy for bureaucracy's sake!

The project problems that were met and overcome in that final phase, were mainly those concerned with human relationships; organising how the people in the decentralised units could be managed both by their local line manager and by their centralised 'process' manager. It was in ITIL and IPW's approach to ensuring clear functional boundaries that the solutions were found. It did not stop the occasional clash of priorities of course but the proof of the pudding is that a successful practical solution was found.

10.14 Conclusions

After just over two and a half years the project was completed successfully. All central and local IT staff had become process driven and responsibilities and tasks within the company had been made very clear. More work was being carried out with fewer people and, importantly, because of the separation of process from organisational structure, future organisational change could take place without fundamentally affecting the way IT services were delivered. And finally, although it had not been one of the original objectives, the project had allowed all five data centres to achieve ISO 9002 certification.

This only happened because of the skill of the people involved and the recognition by the IT managers that implementing Service Management is more than implementing ITIL.

On an occasion of this kind, it becomes more than a moral duty to speak one's mind. It becomes a pleasure
Oscar Wilde
The Importance of Being Earnest

IPW is a trademark of the Quint Wellington Redwood Group and PTT Telecom Automation

An introduction to case studies in Chapters 11 and 12

The final two cases, in which ITIL and PROLIN form the main theme, come from the Netherlands. Both cases concern large-scale organisations responsible for the implementation of social legislation. Both have opted for the ITIL approach combined with the Pro/Helpdesk system and tools supplied by PROLIN. The main difference between them is their history. One (the GAK – the Dutch Industrial Insurance Administration Office) has been using ITIL for some time and added the PROLIN tools along the way. This case study at GAK focuses on measuring the advantages of ITIL. The other (the Detam – Dutch Industrial Insurance Board for the Retail Trade and Tradespeople), started with PROLIN Pro/Helpdesk modules and came into contact with ITIL as a result. Pro/Helpdesk is entirely ITIL-oriented and is extended as ITIL is further developed. The Detam case study mostly concentrates on the justification and implication of support tools.

Justifying and implementing support tools for ITIL

11 Justifying and implementing support tools for ITIL

*This case study was provided by
PROLIN*

11 Justifying and implementing support tools for ITIL

11.1 Introduction

Information Technology and Automation (I&A) departments are hardly ever static. Technological developments are too fast and furious for them to stand still. Sometimes, political and market developments exacerbate the demand for IT specialists in the I&A department to be flexible. At times like that, ITIL can be very useful.

11.2 Where we started from

Peter Reitsma has worked at the Detam for eighteen years. The first fifteen years were fairly quiet. Under the terms of social legislation, retailers and trades people and their employees were simply affiliated with the Detam; there was no alternative, and everyone within the Detam employed the services provided by its own computing centre. There was no need to change this situation. The result was a somewhat static enterprise – call it an 'old style' quango – in which everyone was sure of their jobs (unless they made a real mess of things) everything followed tried and tested procedures and, moreover, the automation department decided what was good for the 'users'. In the last three years that Peter Reitsma has been at the Detam, this situation has changed dramatically.

11.3 Justification: processes of change

Let us sum up a few radical changes that have already taken place or are currently underway.

- The traditional mainframe environment is rapidly making way for client/server and PC LAN/WAN structures. There is a fair chance that the Detam will not have a single mainframe left in a few year's time.

- The Detam employs some 2,600 people (in over thirty branch offices) and has even more PCs and terminals, all of which are regularly required to move.

- Nowadays, politics and the market expect the industrial insurance board to make even more of an effort. It is no longer an established fact that customers traditionally affiliated with the Detam remain so for years on end. They are now free to choose.

- The Detam organisation itself is being divided into more or less autonomous business units, each with its own target.

- The I&A department is certainly part of this trend and will have a few years at the most to establish itself as a competitive supplier of IT services. The department's budget is already being cut if it fails to achieve set expectations. The other Detam units will soon be free to buy their IT services elsewhere.

- And to make things even more complicated; there is a declaration of intent on the table for a merger between Detam and a fellow industrial insurance board of almost the same size, the BVG. If this declaration actually goes through, two highly divergent worlds of I&A will have to be interconnected in the next three to five years.

For top level IT services, one can no longer make do with inadequate or limited tools. What is needed now is the implementation of support tools that allows an integrated approach to basically all internal IT services.

11.4 Orientation: where we wanted to be	These are turbulent times for the IT specialists at the Detam, an organisation that is crying out for structure and management. This is why what we now call configuration management and a Help desk were started up about three years ago. Peter Reitsma is in charge of the Help desk team at the Detam. It did not take him long, however, to realise that the tools he had at his disposal for the management of the Help desk were inadequate for the job. His colleague Donald Wijsman, head of the configuration management team, came to the same conclusion in his work; a lot of effort and work for an unsatisfactory result. Reitsma: `It was obvious something would have to change. We decided not to build anything ourselves, but to have a look around the market. Our research was thorough and, ultimately, we plumped for PROLIN's Pro/Helpdesk. An important reason for our choice was that Pro/Helpdesk covers both the Help Desk functions and configuration management. The system can also be extended, for example, with problem and change management. And finally, Pro/Helpdesk is compatible with Oracle technology, which the Detam is using more and more.

11.5 Implementation: how we got there

Early in 1994, it was decided to buy Pro/Helpdesk, but it took another nine months before implementation was in fact started. The program required a Unix machine that Detam did not have, and in an organisation such as Detam this meant that the whole authorisation process had to be gone through all over again. As it was also considered better to wait until the holidays were over, actual implementation did not start under September 1994, and a very energetic start it was too. A task force classified the hardware, software and network systems in a way that both the Help Desk and the configuration management will be able to work with for years to come. They were assisted by the Prolin consultants, who could draw on experience gained in previous jobs. The final classification consisted of two screens containing basic information about such things as type of equipment, serial number, date of purchase, supplier, service provider, guarantee number, price, cost centre and site. For Help Desk functions, type and site are the two most important items.

The database itself was loaded in October 1994. 'We decided from the outset not to convert data from our old tools,' says Mr Reitsma. 'The old data was far from complete and contained too many incorrect records. That is why we set up an action plan and made available the necessary funds to re-enter all data, this time correctly. That was quite a job, all the more so because the equipment was divided among more than thirty sites. All in all, we are talking about more than 7,000 hardware units, a number that is growing daily.'

11.6 Where we are now

In October 1994, three people had a full-time job loading the database, assisted by about a dozen volunteers at the different sites. Most of the work had to be done early in the morning or on the free Saturday. As Donald Wijsman comments; 'fortunately, Pro/Helpdesk can be combined with an effective bar-code system. That October, all hardware modules were given a bar-code sticker linking them to the background information in the database. Furthermore, all offices in thirty or more branches were charted and given their own bar-code, which makes it very easy to link types of equipment to their site using a hand-held terminal. Very useful for both Help Desk functions and periodic inventories.

'These inventories are necessary to keep the database up-to-date. Don't ask how or why, but computers and peripheral equipment manage to disappear now and then, if only to the supplier's for repairs. Appropriate steps must of course be taken, ranging from finding the missing machine to buying replacement systems.

So far, all we have done is input the *hardware* into the database. The software and network systems still have to be done. Preparations for this are nearly complete, so we can soon start loading them into the database. Separate registration is also being considered for critical hardware modules.'

That is not the end of the implementation process, however. Attention has now turned to other functions, such as the Help Desk. Detam is already looking to expand these basic systems by solving problems in advance and guiding change management. Different kinds of software distribution are also being considered. Although Detam still has a long way to go in its support tool implementation, it has laid a strong foundation to build on in the near future.

11.7 Where we go from here: on the trail of ITIL

Once it had chosen Pro/Helpdesk, the Detam was on the trail of ITIL, since PROLIN uses ITIL as a guideline for its products. `I had heard of ITIL, but I did not know much about it', Wijsman admits. `PROLIN told us about ITIL's potential, as did Bull, our main hardware supplier, at almost the same time. The result was that the board allocated a significant budget for a study of the potential and the benefit of using ITIL within our organisation. This enabled us to attend courses and seminars, conduct internal research etc. The situation as it stands is that we take ITIL on board and carry on in the same direction.' Reitsma adds that the board has approved the ITIL route. 'I think that's a vital point, because you can't make these kinds of decisions without management support. I believe that the ITIL route has to be accepted by the entire organisation, or it would not succeed. Some options are being kept open due the impending merger. As far as I know, our new partner, the BVG, is not yet working with ITIL, but I think they'll have to change that. It's already hard to oversee the configuration, and it's becoming even more complex. We believe ITIL to be an excellent method for controlling and channelling this complicated material. I can well imagine that the integration, which will have to follow the merger, will be conducted on the basis of ITIL.'

11.8 Users become customers

Furthermore, the Service Organisation has been operating within the Detam for just under two years. This is a platform for periodic consultations between representatives of all sections of the facility management company, and, although the entire Library is not yet available during these consultations, this platform is assuming more and more ITIL 'features'. It seems obvious that this will become more structured in the not-too-distant future.

The Detam is undergoing radical processes of change which are crying out for methods and tools to manage them. This concerns not only management of the technical side of the matter. Detam's I&A department will soon have to measure up to other potential (commercial) suppliers, and when it does, it will require an adequate organisation and approach to the work. The Detam's facility management company has already travelled some way down this new road. Donald Wijsman couches the situation in a short but typical sentence: 'We don't talk about 'users' any more. They have become 'our customers'. Things could not be better.

Measuring advantages gained from using ITIL

12 Measuring advantages gained from using ITIL

*This case study was provided by
PROLIN*

12   Measuring advantages gained from using ITIL

12.1   Introduction

The Dutch Industrial Insurance Schemes (GAK) is now reaping the benefits of four years of ITIL efforts. The past few years have been full of ups and downs, and those involved are well aware of the fact that what has been achieved now is but a milestone on a long road yet to be travelled. Systematic measurement allows continuous adjustment of processes and yields indications of the advantages of using ITIL. But that is all they are – indications; ITIL is only one of the factors that influence improvement processes.

Everyone in the Netherlands knows the GAK, an organisation responsible for the administrative paperwork of about fifteen industrial insurance boards. They implement social legislation by collecting premiums, on the one hand, and by providing benefits like unemployment, sickness and disablement benefits. All in all, a considerable number of the Dutch employers, as well as hundreds of thousands of unemployed and disabled people, come into contact with the GAK. This means that millions of people are involved and the concomitant paperwork is extremely extensive. The GAK employs 16,000 people, who work in the headquarters in Amsterdam and in thirty district offices. Almost all of them have a PC or terminal on their desks. All terminals and PCs are integrated into a standardised national network linking five computing centres, directed by the R&I (computing centres and infrastructure) department.

12.2   Where we started from and what triggered the change

`Some five years ago, the need for a more structured approach towards IT services arose in this R&I department,' says Jos London, who supervises the team responsible for the optimisation of business processes. 'This was not because a lot of complaints about quality were received from people within the organisation, but rather as a result of the growing awareness that IT services were, and still are, of crucial importance to the GAK. If, say, a computer in an industrial company breaks down, they can just go on making products and catch up the administrative backlog later. But things are different in an organisation like ours. If one of the main computers breaks down, thousands of our people are unproductive, because production is impossible. And what's worse, if this breakdown continues, hundreds or thousands of people will receive their benefits too late. This is bad for our name and must be prevented at all costs.'

12.3 How we started

This awareness, fed by advice from a consultant, led the GAK to ITIL. London explains: 'The ITIL approach was welcomed with open arms. At last we had a method to channel all kinds of processes; at last we had a theory that expressed what we had always thought but could never put a finger on. Although, as I said, we were under no pressure to have the computing centre function more efficiently run, ITIL was still an eye-opener for management. The ITIL books were studied fervently and consulted all the time to solve problems. Mind you, I'm talking about the first stage of ITIL experience, in the early 90s. In those days, most IT people were still up in their ivory towers, with an attitude of 'I manage a brilliant network, but it is such a nuisance that other people make it unstable owing to their unpredictable behaviour'. This was also the attitude with which ITIL was approached. I'm exaggerating a bit, but ITIL became a hype for a relatively small group; there was not enough link to the shop-floor, to the people that actually had to render the services. In this stage ITIL became well-known in the organisation, but there was too little integration of ITIL in our business process. After two years of experimenting this way, ITIL seemed to die a slow death.'

12.4 How we got out

The approach taken in the second phase, which started in the middle of 1993, was totally different. 'We realised that ITIL was not a panacea and, what's more important, we understand that we had to gear the things ITIL offered to our own organisation,' reasons London. 'We established a team to guide the ITIL process, evaluated the strengths and weaknesses of our organisation and the tools available to use, and sifted out the most relevant ITIL themes. We soon found out that we already had some elements, such as change management and software distribution. All we needed to do was interconnect those elements and to extend with other elements.'

The GAK has also learnt to employ ITIL in a more practice-oriented manner. London: 'We de-theorised ITIL within the organisation in favour of simply completing and implementing. And not just for the happy few, but for everyone. In addition, we constantly evaluated and checked, so that all computing centre employees soon learned the ITIL approach. Consequently, everyone could see for themselves that the new approach generated improvement.' On the other hand, employees did have to change their working methods. Previously, IT specialists used to work mostly in isolation; they all worked on their own little islands. But with the new approach, the work environment is much more open. What's more, everybody has to make a record of what they intend to do in order to improve the co-ordination of the activities. This met with some resistance initially, but that soon changed once they saw the improvement.'

12.5 Measuring

In the first phase, up to 1993, results were rarely measured. Subsequently, however, the GAK started collecting data systematically, particularly regarding the degree of availability of IT systems. Six-month plans were drawn up and monthly reports written on the actual situation. Responsibility was allocated for the plans and monthly reports required for all the processes (such as configuration management, Help Desk, problem and change management). 'We made a division according to process organisation on the one hand and process implementation on the other,' said London. 'Process organisation concerns procedures that exist or are to be introduced, how much is known about them, and who is responsible for their implementation. In addition, reports are written on everyday matters, such as the number of failures reported to the Help Desk in the past month, the nature of the failures, how they were solved and how long it took to solve them. We also have a similar system for other processes, such as what changes have been made to the system (change management), at whose request and with what result. We started using checklists for this which derive largely from ITIL.'

At the end of 1994, the GAK succeeded in organising most of the processes in such a way that measurement was possible and useful. Initially, different information systems were used for each process. As a result, the information collected was inconsistent, making control inefficient and difficult. So the GAK started looking for a system for integrating the processes in order to improve control.

12.6 How we got where we wanted to be

In the fourth quarter of 1994, most of the operational processes were redesigned. Each process was supported by an information system and that worked quite well. Nevertheless the improvements once again seemed to come to a halt. The main reason was that the GAK had many different information systems supporting the business processes. The co-ordination was insufficient and it was far from easy to realise consistency in the information flows. Managing the processes and the integration of processes, became more and more difficult.

Another aspect was the intensification of the information system, partly to show that the new approach really provides more efficiency and effectiveness, partly to gain an even better understanding of the relation between processes of change and the desires of clients. An integrated (and integrating) tool was needed to support all processes in order to obtain more extensive, consistent information. This tool was found in the form of the Pro/Helpdesk from PROLIN of Amsterdam.

'In our search for suitable tools, we found that there are many suppliers in this field', says London. `But most packages covered only part of the subject and/or were not ITIL-oriented. Pro/Helpdesk is based on ITIL and provides an integrated approach towards all elements. Furthermore, PROLIN was prepared to help us to co-ordinate the modules exactly to our own requirements. PROLIN made use of our experience in this field in the development of the product'.

This is not the place for an extensive discussion of the PROLIN system but we do want to give a brief overview of Pro/Helpdesk, because, contrary to what the name suggests, it includes much more than Help Desk functions. It consists of the following modules:

- configuration management
- Help Desk management
- problem management
- change management
- software control & distribution
- service level management.

All modules are integrated, but can also be used separately, so it is possible to install the system in phases. 'We have also added elements to the software system using our experience and expertise in the field of ITIL,' explains London. 'Pro/Helpdesk is extremely flexible, aimed at future developments and, partly because of that, suitable for the GAK. It meets our requirements for more comprehensive and, particularly, consistent information. This has given new impetus to our ITIL processes.'

12.7   Lessons learned

At the GAK, process measurement is always geared towards ascertaining the availability of IT systems. That availability must, of course, be optimal, preferably 100%. However, that maximum is probably unattainable as our organisation is constantly undergoing processes of change, which naturally also affect availability. After all, when someone in the organisation wants a new application package, it is by no means always available. London explains, 'We attach great importance to the wishes of our clients, the people who work with the IT systems. We work from the bottom up to ensure that our organisation is as prepared as it can be and to keep availability of IT systems as high as possible. In addition, we also work from the top down, ie we consult closely with our clients in order to take stock of their wishes. When working from the bottom up, ITIL is ideal; for the top-down method, the clients come first, and they are not interested in ITIL or ISO. They simply want to see results.'

London does not cite any exact figures (they would be of no use to other organisations anyway), but he does say that availability has increased to a considerable extent lately. 'But I would not go so far as to attribute that improvement entirely to ITIL,' says London. 'There are other factors involved. For example, the technical services have sharpened up, and PCs and other computer equipment have become far more reliable in the course of time. You see, if such machines simply do not break down any more, the degree of availability automatically approaches the 100% mark.'

12.8   Where we go from here

It is impossible to imagine the IT department of the GAK organisation without the ITIL approach. London even considers the approach to be of 'vital importance'. A major shift has taken place within the GAK with respect to the perception of ITIL. Initially, ITIL was approached primarily from a technical point of view, to solve technical problems. Nowadays, ITIL has been put in a service and business economics perspective, tilting the matrix 90°: the focus is not on software, hardware and networks, but on providing services to our customers with their specific requirements. Jos London expects this service/business economic perspective to gain in relevance in the next few years.

'Certain trends within the GAK are leading towards the IT organisation becoming more independent. This inevitably comes with a certain degree of professionalism in the relationship between the R&D department as service supplier and the other GAK user departments. How does the user, the customer, perceive the computing centre, what are the requirements of the customer, what do they want to pay for them? This implies that we have to pay more attention to their requirements and to making facilities available to them. We cannot go on simply reacting to developments, we must also anticipate new developments and the customer requirements that ensue from these developments. The ITIL approach has rendered this possible.'

Annex A
Profiles of consultancies involved

Pink Elephant
F.I. Group plc
Quint Wellington Redwood
Ultracomp Ltd
Prolin Automation

Pink Elephant

Profile in outline

Pink Elephant offers integrated services on management and exploitation of Information Technology to all organisations whose business processes are dependent on IT. The company is specialised in technical, organisational and business management of computer and information centres, at operational, tactical and strategic levels.

In addition, Pink Elephant offers many services related to IT organisational structure, consultancy and IT management. Assignments in these fields range from the establishment, staffing and technical management of computer and information centres, control of networks and office automation, consultancy, facilities management and outsourcing, education (in relation to IT management), through to executing interim and long-term line and project management functions

Through full adoption and via contributions to CCTA's development of the IT Infrastructure Library (ITIL) management method, Pink Elephant has helped to promote ITIL as the *de facto* standard for IT infrastructure management.

Pink Elephant has fifteen years of experience in the management of computer and information centres, is the business partner in IT management for several multi-national companies, and employs more than 950 staff.

The Pink Elephant Group is part of the Roccade Informatica Groep.

Company name and address

Pink Elephant Group
Public Sector bv
Postbus 106
2270 AC Voorburg

Telephone + 31 70 304 77 77
Fax + 31 70 335 13 57

F.I. Group plc (FI)

Profile in outline

FI offers a variety of managed IT services to support its customers which include some of the largest blue chip companies in the UK. FI works to suit each customer's needs through partnerships, through managed services and training and through the recruitment of computer personnel.. It's MAINSTAY application support and maintenance service is a market leader in the UK.

FI strives for excellence in customer service, quality of work, innovation and flexibility. Its reputation has been noted by such gurus as Tom Peters and Charles Handy, and was reflected in recent years by a British Standards quality accreditation (BS EN ISO 9001).

FI has been involved in ITIL since its inception, reviewing and commenting on several of the ITIL books prior to publication. FI is an accredited trainer for service support and delivery and has more than twenty accredited ITIL consultants. FI's MAINSTAY product manager sits on the management board of the ITIMF and FI has provided speakers at a number of ITIMF forums.

For further information please contact:

F.I.GROUP plc
Campus 300
Maylands Avenue
Hemel Hempstead
Hertfordshire HP2 7TQ

Tel: 01442 238300
Fax: 01442 238400

Quint Wellington Redwood

Profile in outline

Quint Wellington Redwood is a group of international organisational improvement companies. It specialises in providing practical help and guidance to the managers who are directly responsible to their business partners for the development and delivery of Information Technology services. It also understands the need for those services to make a measurable contribution to the business value chain and for that contribution to be recognised.

The Group focuses on the five main areas of work in which its professionally qualified consultants have extensive practical experience; service management (service support and delivery), sourcing, service and technical architectures, quality and information economics

The *independent* advice and guidance for which the company is highly regarded includes audits, health checks, education and training, consultancy, tool selection and implementation and interim management. It may be at a strategic level, helping to create new service lifecycle relationships, or in operational mode, assisting with the setting up of improved support processes and procedures. In either case, although an assessment of the present state will be necessary, what is most required is a clear and firm presentation of the actions and resources needed to move from the current position to that chosen by the client. Quint Wellington Redwood therefore specialises in providing just that; not simply concentrating on *what* needs to be done but on exactly *how* the changes are to be successfully negotiated and measured.

In assisting its clients to progress satisfactorily through the four phases of organisational improvement – analyse, unfreeze, reconfigure and re-freeze – Quint Wellington Redwood employs its own unique understanding of the service management processes. These are embodied within the company's process models which, together with their associated process relationship and data flow diagrams and descriptions, have proved their worth in a wide variety of situations. Two of these are described in this book.

Company name and address

For further information, please contact:

For the UK, Ireland and the British Commonwealth
Quint Wellington Redwood (UK) Ltd.
Suite 18 North Oxford Business Centre
Lakesmere Close
Oxford
OX5 1LG

Tel: +44 (0) 1865 370501
Fax: +44 (0) 1865 370502

For the Caribbean, Central and South America
Fervoro Consultants n.v.
Kaya Wilson Goddett 33-35
Pietermaai
Curaçao
Netherlands Antilles

Tel: +599 9 656169
Fax: +599 9 656391

For Mainland Europe, North America and the Rest of the World
Quint Wellington Redwood Nederland b.v.
Group Headquarters
Emmaplein 2
1075 AW Amsterdam
The Netherlands

Tel: +31 (0) 20 6761600
Fax:+31 (0) 20 6761700

Ultracomp Ltd

Profile in outline

Ultracomp is a leading supplier of Service Management products, consultancy services and training. Since its formation in 1981, Ultracomp's strategy has been to focus its energy and skills on helping IT providers improve the delivery and support of services to their users.

Ultracomp has a well established and evolutionary product development strategy for all of its Service Management tools. The Red Box Service Management System represents the latest generation of Ultracomp's product strategy and provides complementary applications for Service Management.

Consultancy and training are an essential part of Ultracomp's Service Management portfolio. This, together with Ultracomp's product strategy, provides a complete service to client organisations. Indeed, Ultracomp is one of the leading suppliers of training for the ISEB's (Information Systems Examination Board) Certificate of Proficiency in IT Infrastructure Management.

Ultracomp is at the forefront of the move towards Service Management methods in the UK. It has worked closely with CCTA contributing to the production of the IT Infrastructure Library – ITIL. These guidelines for professional IT management have been adopted by many organisations throughout Europe and the UK.

Ultracomp designs and develops its product set at its UK development centre in Bracknell. With over 100 staff Ultracomp has built up an excellent reputation for the delivery of software, consultancy and training.

Ultracomp's customers include many of the largest computer users in both the commercial and public sectors. Nearly 600 organisations rely on Ultracomp products and services in the UK, the Netherlands, Australia, South East Asia and South Africa.

Company name and address

For further information please contact:

Marketing Manager
Ultracomp Ltd
Ultracomp House
Pinehill Road
Crowthorne
Berks RG45 7JD

Tel: 01344 779333
Fax: 01344 779385

Prolin Automation

Profile in outline

Prolin Automation is a relatively young company whose history is characterised by very strong and continuous growth. Founded in 1987, the company has grown into an international organisation with distributors and resellers in many different parts of the world.

Prolin Automation has based its IT Service Management tool PROLIN IT Service Manager (originally known as Pro/Helpdesk) on the guidance contained in ITIL. As the new name implies the took supports problem management, change management, configuration management, software control and distribution and service level management.

PROLIN IT Service Manager has been developed with Oracle Case Tools in the Oracle RDBMS environment and runs over more than 80 different platforms. PROLINS not only have the resources and expertise to help ensure the successful installation and implementation of their tools, they also provide training for beginners and advanced system users.

PROLIN's philosophy is to be more than just a supplier of tools by forming partnerships with their customers. The products that Prolin offers closely fit the needs and demands of organisations with a very complex and extensive IT infrastructure. So it is no surprise that various organisations from the Fortune top 1000 are Prolin clients.

For further information please contact:

PROLIN
Van Diemenstraat 200
1013 CN Amsterdam

Tel: +31 20 530 1600
Fax: +31 20 530 1611

email: prolin@prolin.nl

PROLIN Benelux NV
Contact: Katleen Baeten
Phone: +32.2.716.4030
Fax: +32.2.716.4727
kbaeten@prolin.nl

For USA - PROLIN Software Inc.
Contact: Mr. Arjen J. Pront
Phone: +1.415.854.7489
Fax: +1.415 854 7537

IT Infrastructure Library
IT Service Management Case Studies
ISBN 0 11 330676 8

CORRECTION

Page 159, line 38: the telephone number of Stichting Exin should read:
(+31/0) 2344 811

Further information and associated guidance

Useful contacts

This book of case studies is part of the IT Infrastructure Library (ITIL). ITIL is managed on behalf of CCTA by Stichting Exin, the Institute for Information Science. If you would like further information on any aspect of ITIL, they can be contacted at:

Exin
Sovereign House
Botolph Street
Norwich NR3 1DN
United Kingdom

Tel: (+44/0) 1603 695172
Fax: (+44/0) 1603 695174
e-mail: itil@exin.nl

An ITIL home page is available on the World Wide Web, at www.exin.nl/itil, which will carry news, information and links for those interested in IT Service Management.

The ITIL books themselves are only a part of the 'ITIL philosophy'; the guidance is supported by training, consultancy and software tools. These are available from many suppliers, not only those who have contributed the articles in this book. The ITIL-based qualifications mentioned in several of the case studies in this book are available for managers, practitioners and at an introductory/familiarisation level. Information is available from the examination bodies:

Stichting Exin	Information Systems
Postbus 19147	Examination Board
3501 DC Utrecht	London W1M 9FJ
Netherlands	United Kingdom

Tel: (+31/0) 30 234811   Tel: (+44/0) 171 637 2040

While the case studies in this book give some idea of the problems others have faced and the benefits possible from an ITIL approach to IT Service Management, they will not, of course, cover all the questions. It is always useful to meet and talk with others in a similar position, or those who have already done what you are setting out to do. Helpful contacts and the chance to discuss appropriate topics are offered by the ITIMF. Established as the user group for ITIL, they offer their members an invaluable forum for Service Management professionals;

including relevant seminars on Service Management topics and an annual conference. Contact them at:

For Benelux	For South Africa & Zimbabwe
ITIMF	ITIMF
Postbus 188	PO Box 69362
9700 AD	Bryanston
Groningen	2021
Netherlands	South Africa

Tel: (+31/0) 50 85 1111 Tel: (+27) 11 8071080

For UK and elsewhere
ITIMF
1A Taverners Square
Silver Road
Norwich NR3 4SY

Tel: 01603 767181

The ITIMF also publishes the ITIL 'Pocketbook' – a handy pocket-sized guide to the core ITIL disciplines.

Further reading

Detailed guidance on the individual IT Service Management functions can be found in the individual ITIL books within the *Service Support* and *Service Delivery* sets. Those considering implementing ITIL may also be interested in some of the books within the *Managers* set:

> *IT Services Organisation*
> *Planning and Control*
> *Customer Liaison*

Also worthy of specific mention is the guide aimed at implementing ITIL with small IT organisations, *ITIL Practices in small IT units.*

The following CCTA volumes provide further information on the topics covered by these case studies. These are published by HMSO and available from the address shown below:

Management of Risk

Introduction to the Management of Risk
ISBN: 0 11 330648 2

Management of Programme Risk
ISBN: 0 11 330672 5

Introduction to Managing Project Risk
ISBN: 0 11 330671 7

Management of Project Risk
ISBN: 0 11 330636 9

PRINCE

For managing individual projects within a programme the PRINCE® method is recommended. The PRINCE Manuals are available from NCC Blackwell, 108 Cowley Road, Oxford, OX4 0JF.

PRINCE Reference Manuals (a five volume set comprising: Introduction to PRINCE, PRINCE Management Guide, PRINCE Technical Guide, PRINCE Quality Guide, PRINCE Configuration Management Guide).
ISBN: 1 85554 012 6

Also available from HMSO:

PRINCE – An Outline
ISBN: 0 11 330599 0

All ITIL books are published by HMSO and are available from ITIMF, in the UK, Benelux and South Africa (see above) or HMSO (see below). In many countries throughout the world, local agents supply ITIL and other HMSO publications. For advice on how best to obtain the books in other countries contact Exin or HMSO.

HMSO Publications Centre
PO Box 276
London SW8 5DT

Tel: 0171 873 9090
Fax: 0171 873 8200

Glossary

application software	An information system that supports a specific business function, such as personnel management or order processing.
architecture	The overall, complete design of, for example, an IT infrastructure, or a building; used in this volume to describe a framework for organisational change.
asset	Component of a business process. Assets can include people, accommodation, computer systems, networks, paper records, fax machines.
BCM	Business Continuity Management.
BCS	British Computer Society.
benchmark	Comparison of performance of a function, process or activity typically between an external organisation and your organisation.
business process	A group of business activities undertaken by an organisation in pursuit of a common goal. Typical business processes include receiving orders, marketing services, selling products, delivering services, distributing products, invoicing for services, accounting for money received. A business process will usually depend on several business functions for support, eg IT, personnel, accommodation. A business process will rarely operate in isolation, ie other business processes will depend on it and it will depend on other processes.
capability	The aggregation of the organisation, people, processes and technology which provides an enterprise with the ability to achieve business goals and satisfy stakeholders.
capacity	Computing and telecommunications power and data storage space: the capacity to process computer transactions and store data which matches the business requirements of the enterprise.
CCTA	The Government Centre for Information Systems.
client/server	An IT architecture in which application processing is partitioned between two separate computers, one a client and one a server. The client requests services across a telecommunications link from the server which performs the requirements of the client.

Configuration Item (CI)	A component of an IT infrastructure – or an item, such as a request for change, associated with an IT infrastructure – which is (or is to be) under the control of configuration management. CIs may vary widely in complexity, size and type – from an entire system (including all hardware software and documentation) to a single module or a minor hardware component.
contingency planning	Planning to address unwanted occurrences that may happen at a later time. Traditionally, the term has been used to refer to planning for the recovery of IT systems rather than entire business processes.
disaster recovery planning	A series of processes that focus only upon the recovery processes, principally in response to physical disasters, that are contained within BCM.
Facilities Management	Placing work with an external specialist (see outsourcing).
incident	A single occurrence of deviation from the specification of an IT infrastructure component or an aspect of IT service.
intelligent customer	A general term applied to an organisation when its culture and procedures successfully enable the planning, implementation and use of IS/IT to achieve business objectives. The capability to purchase (as distinct from provide) IT services. The term is often used in relation to the outsourcing of IT/IS.
IS	Information System.
ISEB	Information Systems Examination Board.
ISO 9000	The International Standards Organisation series of standards relating to Quality Management.
ISDN	Integrated Services Digital Network.
IT service management	The totality of providing one or more IT services to business units and of effectively managing the underpinning IT Infrastructure.
IT infrastructure	The hardware, software, organisation, procedures, computer related communications, documentation and skills required to support the provision of IT services.
IT system	In the context of this volume, IT system is used as an embracing term for the hardware and software that serve as the basis for provision of an IT service or services to customers.

IT	Information Technology.
ITIL	The CCTA IT Infrastructure Library – a set of guides on the management and provision of operational IT services.
market testing	Inviting bids from external service providers which are compared on a fair commercial basis with bids to run the same service from the internal provider, to achieve best value for the enterprise.
outsourcing	The process by which functions performed by the organisation are contracted out for operation, on the organisation's behalf, by third parties.
preventive maintenance	Action taken to make subsequent maintenance more efficient and reliable. This includes reverse engineering.
PRINCE®	PRojects IN a Controlled Environment, the CCTA project management method. PRINCE® is a registered trademark of CCTA, the Government Centre for Information Systems.
problem	The underlying cause of multiple occurrences of incidents; also, a serious incident.
release	A collection of new and/or changed configuration items which are tested and introduced into the live environment together.
Request for Change (RFC)	A form or screen, used to record details of a request for a change to any component of an IT Infrastructure or any aspect of IT services.
risk	The chance exposure to the adverse consequences of future events. A measure of the exposure to which an organisation may be subjected. This is a combination of the likelihood of a business disruption occurring and the possible loss that may result from such disruption.
service provider	A third party organisation supplying services or products to customers.
Service Level Agreement (SLA)	A formal statement of service characteristics between a demander and supplier of services.
software lifecycle	The lifetime of a software system from conception to decommissioning. Software lifecycle includes enhancement and maintenance following delivery.
software (development) method	A systematic way of performing part or all of the processes involved in a lifecycle model or stage (for example, the requirements stage, or design stage).

Printed in the United Kingdom for HMSO
Dd301202 4/96 C10 G3397 10170